the

ILLUSTRATED
HISTORIES

of

EVERYDAY
BEHAVIOR

the
ILLUSTRATED
HISTORIES
of
EVERYDAY
BEHAVIOR

{ *Discover the True Stories Behind*
the 64 Most Popular Daily Rituals }

by Laura Hetherington
Illustrated *by* Rebecca Pry

WHALEN
BOOK·WORKS

Kennebunkport, Maine

THE ILLUSTRATED HISTORIES
OF EVERYDAY BEHAVIOR

13-digit ISBN: 978-1-951-51103-6
10-digit ISBN: 1-951-51103-4

This book may be ordered by mail from the publisher. Please include $5.99 for postage and handling. Please support your local bookseller first!

Books published by Whalen Book Works are available at special discounts when purchased in bulk. For more information, please email us at info@whalenbookworks.com.

Whalen Book Works
68 North Street
Kennebunkport, ME 04046

www.whalenbookworks.com

Cover and interior design by Melissa Gerber
Typography: Caveat, Adobe Caslon, Bell MT, Calligraphr, DinPro

Printed in China
1 2 3 4 5 6 7 8 9 0

First Edition

This book is dedicated to Charlie.

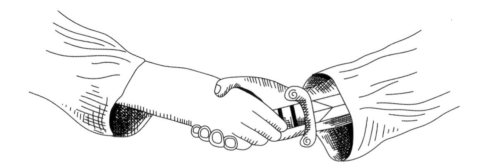

CONTENTS

"The stories are there if you listen."
—Kate Tempest

INTRODUCTION

Across every culture there are spoken and unspoken customs that unify the human experience. Daily behaviors and common rituals are responsible for communication, connection, and conflict. When we celebrate the birth of a new life, our joy is the joy of centuries. When we order a round for the table or kiss someone we love, we're keeping a bit of history alive, whether we know it or not. When we clash and feud, this too is born from an age-old desire: we want to make the right decisions, and we care enough to fight for it.

We've all wondered if someone saw our message and if we should text again. People from all eras share the tendency to fall victim to our insecurities. We share the urge to establish familiar traditions, and brand-new forms of expression. Some of these everyday behaviors came from different practices around the world trying to accomplish the same thing. Some were born of necessity, and some started as marketing campaigns.

Our rituals signal that we care, and they signal when we don't. They signal that we're tired in the morning, that we're coming to the party, and that you should slow down because there's a police car ahead. Enjoy the fascinating stories behind these remarkable sixty-four and appreciate your next handshake a little more.

- THE TRADITION OF -
SHAKING HANDS
SEALING THE DEAL

ANCIENT IMAGES OF HANDSHAKES HAVE BEEN FOUND IN ART AND SCULPTURE DATING BACK TO FIFTH-CENTURY GREECE. THE HANDSHAKE IS BELIEVED TO HAVE ORIGINATED AS A GESTURE OF PEACE, AS IT REQUIRED PRESENTING A WEAPONLESS RIGHT HAND TO THE OTHER PERSON IN GOOD FAITH. IT IS EVEN RUMORED THAT THE SHAKING MOTION WAS A WAY OF TURNING LOOSE ANY HIDDEN WEAPONS UP THE OTHER'S SLEEVE!

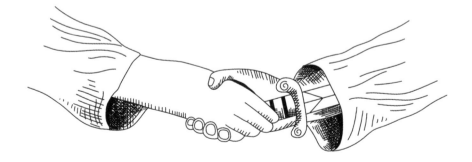

HISTORY SHOWS EVIDENCE OF THE HANDSHAKE BEING USED AS A WAY TO **CONFIRM DEALS OR ALLIANCES IN POLITICS**. IN ANCIENT ROME IT WAS ALSO DEPICTED AS A WAY TO **SEAL MARRIAGE** BETWEEN A MAN AND A WOMAN, OR TO SERVE A CEREMONIAL PURPOSE.

THE HANDSHAKE SPREAD AS AN INFORMAL GREETING AMONG THE QUAKERS IN THE SEVENTEENTH CENTURY AS AN ALTERNATIVE TO TIPPING ONE'S HAT. TODAY WE EMPHASIZE THE IMPORTANCE OF A SOLID HANDSHAKE FOR MAKING A GOOD IMPRESSION AT A JOB INTERVIEW AND WHEN MEETING SOMEONE FOR THE FIRST TIME. IT NOT ONLY REPRESENTS TRUST AND CONTRACT, BUT SIGNIFIES FRIENDSHIP, COMRADERY, AND RESPECT.

TOO FIRM

TOO WET

JUST RIGHT

SPLITTING THE BILL

PAYING YOUR WAY

PAYING FOR YOUR OWN PORTION OF THE BILL INSTEAD OF BEING TREATED IS NO WILD IDEA, BUT A TALE CLAIMS THE PRACTICE WAS POPULARIZED BY GERMAN IMMIGRANTS WHO CAME TO PENNSYLVANIA IN THE 1600s AND 1700s.

12

THEY WERE KNOWN AS THE PENNSYLVANIA
DUTCH EVEN THOUGH THEY WEREN'T FROM
THE NETHERLANDS; THIS NAME LIKELY CAME
FROM A VARIATION OF THE WORD DEUTSCH,
THE LANGUAGE THE GERMANS SPOKE. THE
PENNSYLVANIA DUTCH SUPPOSEDLY HELD
PRIDE IN PAYING FOR THEMSELVES AND NOT
OWING DEBTS, SO THE PRACTICE BECAME
KNOWN AS **GOING DUTCH**.

THERE IS EVEN AN 1873 EDITORIAL IN *THE BALTIMORE AMERICAN*
THAT ADVISES USING THE **DUTCH TREAT** TO DISCOURAGE AMERICANS
WHO DRINK IN EXCESS, POSING THAT YOU MIGHT BE LESS LIKELY TO
OVERINDULGE IF YOU'RE FOOTING THE BILL.

- THE TRADITION OF -
BRINGING A TEACHER AN APPLE
POLISHING YOUR GRADE

ON THE AMERICAN FRONTIER, MANY COMMUNITIES WERE RESPONSIBLE FOR ESTABLISHING THEIR OWN SCHOOLS. TOWNSPEOPLE AND STUDENTS HELPED WITH SCHOOLHOUSE UPKEEP, AND OFTEN PROVIDED FOOD AND HOUSING FOR THEIR TEACHERS.

AS A WAY OF SAYING THANKS, FARMERS GAVE PRODUCE TO SCHOOLTEACHERS, MANY OF WHOM WERE UNMARRIED WOMAN WHO RECEIVED LITTLE PAY. A **BASKET OF APPLES** MADE A PRACTICAL GIFT TO SHOW APPRECIATION.

SUCH A KISS UP!

THE APPLE ALSO SERVES AS A SYMBOL OF KNOWLEDGE IN THE STORY OF ADAM AND EVE. GIVING TEACHERS AN APPLE BECAME SO POPULAR THAT IN THE 1900s THE TERM **APPLE-POLISHER** WAS USED TO DESCRIBE A KISS-UP. AS BING CROSBY SANG IN 1939, "AN APPLE FOR THE TEACHER WILL ALWAYS DO THE TRICK."

CALLING SHOTGUN

CLAIMING YOUR SEAT

CALLING SHOTGUN IS SAID TO HAVE ORIGINATED IN THE WILD WEST, WHEN TRAVEL COULD BE QUITE DANGEROUS. AN ARMED PERSON SAT BESIDE THE DRIVER AND ACTED AS A STAGECOACH GUARD, SHOOTING AT ANY ANIMALS OR THIEVES WHO POSED DANGER.

REFERENCE TO **SHOTGUN-WIELDING GUARDS** ON THE SO-CALLED BOX OF THE STAGECOACH CAN BE FOUND IN NEWS PUBLICATIONS FROM THE LATE 1800s, AND A CHARACTER IS SAID TO BE RIDIN' SHOTGUN IN THE SHORT STORY "THE FIGHTING FOOL" BY DANE COOLIDGE, PUBLISHED IN 1918.

THE PHRASE CONTINUED TO GROW IN POPULARITY ONCE IT APPEARED IN WESTERN FILMS LIKE **STAGECOACH** (1939) AND **RIDING SHOTGUN** (1954). TODAY, CALLING SHOTGUN IS A SORT OF GAME TO DETERMINE WHO GETS TO SIT IN THE SPACIOUS PASSENGER SEAT OF A CAR.

PRACTICING THE GOLDEN RULE

TREAT OTHERS AS YOU WANT TO BE TREATED

WE'VE ALL HEARD SOME ITERATION OF "TREAT OTHERS AS YOU WANT TO BE TREATED," *OTHERWISE KNOWN AS THE GOLDEN RULE. THOUGH IT IS COMMONLY ASSOCIATED WITH THE BIBLE, THE GOLDEN RULE IS FOUND IN MANY RELIGIONS AND CULTURES, DATING BACK TO AS EARLY AS ANCIENT EGYPT IN THE TALE OF THE ELOQUENT PEASANT.*

DO UNTO OTHERS

THE ANCIENT INDIAN EPIC MAHABHARATA INCLUDES BOTH **"TREAT OTHERS AS YOU TREAT YOURSELF"** AND **"THIS IS THE SUM OF DUTY: DO NAUGHT UNTO OTHERS WHICH WOULD CAUSE YOU PAIN IF DONE TO YOU."** THE GOLDEN RULE ALSO DATES BACK TO ANCIENT CHINA IN CONFUCIANISM, AND IS PRESENT IN ISLAM, BUDDHISM, CHRISTIANITY, AND JUDAISM.

WHEN WE LOOK AT THE GENERAL PRINCIPLE OF THE GOLDEN RULE, WE SEE IT IN EVEN MORE PLACES THROUGHOUT HISTORY, INCLUDING THE ORAL CONSTITUTION OF THE IROQUOIS CONFEDERACY.

EVEN THE NOTION OF *AN EYE FOR AN EYE*, FROM HAMMURABI'S CODE IN ANCIENT BABYLON REPRESENTS THE **CONCEPT OF RECIPROCITY** BEHIND THE GOLDEN RULE.

- THE TRADITION OF -
PAYING IT FORWARD
SENDING KINDNESS DOWN THE LINE

THE NOTION OF BEING KIND TO OTHERS HAS ALWAYS BEEN AROUND, BUT PAYING IT FORWARD IS THE PRACTICE OF REPAYING AN ACT OF KINDNESS BY DOING SOMETHING KIND FOR SOMEONE ELSE. ONE OF THE FIRST RECORDED WORKS TO EXPLORE THIS CONCEPT IS AN ANCIENT GREEK COMEDY BY MENANDER CALLED **DYSKOLOS** OR, **THE GROUCH,** PERFORMED IN 317 BC.

THE IDEA CONTINUED TO EVOLVE OVER TIME. THERE IS EVEN A LETTER WRITTEN BY **BENJAMIN FRANKLIN** IN 1784, IN WHICH HE ASKS THE RECIPIENT TO REPAY FRANKLIN'S LOAN BY LENDING IT TO ANOTHER MAN SOMEDAY WHO NEEDS IT.

ONE OF THE FIRST TIMES THE ACTUAL WORDS PAY IT FORWARD ARE USED TO DESCRIBE THIS CONCEPT IS IN THE 1916 NOVEL IN THE GARDEN OF DELIGHT BY LILY HARDY HAMMOND: **"YOU DON'T PAY LOVE BACK; YOU PAY IT FORWARD."**

- THE TRADITION OF -
CLINKING GLASSES
TOASTING THE GOOD LIFE

IT IS CUSTOMARY AROUND THE WORLD TO CLINK GLASSES FOR A TOAST, AND ALMOST EVERY COUNTRY HAS SOME ITERATION OF A PHRASE OR RITUAL TO GO ALONG WITH IT. WHETHER IT'S CHEERS, KAMPAI, OR ARRIBA, ABAJO, AL CENTRO Y ADENTRO, THE CEREMONY OF DRINKING IS UNIVERSALLY RECOGNIZED.

ONE POPULAR RUMOR CLAIMS THAT WE CLINK GLASSES BECAUSE THE SOUND WAS A WAY TO **WARD OFF EVIL** SPIRITS BACK IN THE MIDDLE AGES. ANOTHER STORY CLAIMS THAT BY CLINKING GLASSES AND SPILLING INTO THE HOST'S CUP, THE GUEST COULD BE SURE THAT THEIR WINE WASN'T **POISONED**.

IN REALITY, IT LIKELY DEVELOPED AS A NOD TO TOGETHERNESS AND SHARING IN FOOD AND DRINK WITH OTHERS. THE TERM **TOAST** ITSELF ORIGINATED SOMETIME IN THE ELIZABETHAN

ERA, WHEN PIECES OF STALE BREAD OR TOAST WERE ADDED TO GLASSES OF WINE THAT WERE OF POOR QUALITY OR ACIDIC TASTE. THE BREAD IMPROVED THE TASTE OF THE WINE, AND BECOME SOFT ENOUGH TO EAT AFTERWARDS, AVOIDING WASTE.

- THE TRADITION OF -
PROPOSING WITH A DIAMOND

A DIAMOND IS FOREVER

WE MUST GO HOME, I LEFT MY IRON RING ON.

ENGAGEMENT RINGS CAN BE TRACED BACK TO ANCIENT TIMES, BUT THEY DIDN'T ALWAYS FEATURE A DIAMOND. IN ANCIENT ROME IT WAS COMMON TO HAVE TWO ENGAGEMENT RINGS: AN **IRON** ONE THAT WOULD BE WORN AROUND THE HOUSE, AND A **GOLD** ONE TO WEAR IN PUBLIC OR AT SPECIAL OCCASIONS.

IT WAS ARCHDUKE MAXIMILIAN I OF AUSTRIA WHO USED ONE OF THE FIRST NOTED DIAMOND ENGAGEMENT RINGS IN 1477. HE PROPOSED TO MARY OF BURGUNDY WITH **A RING FEATURING DIAMONDS IN THE SHAPE OF AN M**. THIS BEGAN THE TREND OF ADDING PRECIOUS GEMS AND STONES TO ENGAGEMENT RINGS AMONG THE NOBLE CLASS.

THE DIAMOND ENGAGEMENT RING WAS SOLIDIFIED AS THE GO-TO CHOICE BY THE 1947 **DE BEERS MINING COMPANY** CAMPAIGN, WITH THE FAMOUS SLOGAN A DIAMOND IS FOREVER.

THE CAMPAIGN SHOWED DIAMONDS WORN BY MOVIE STARS, AND EVEN FEATURED LECTURERS WHO VISITED HIGH SCHOOLS TO TALK UP DIAMONDS. THEY AIMED TO MAKE DIAMONDS A SYMBOL OF ETERNITY, INDISTINGUISHABLE FROM THE IDEA OF MARRIAGE, AND THEY SUCCEEDED.

- THE TRADITION OF -
APPLAUDING

GIVE THEM A HAND

HUMAN BEINGS HAVE BEEN APPLAUDING FOREVER.
IT'S A NATURAL WAY OF COMMUNICATING WITHOUT LANGUAGE: EVEN BABIES DO IT! IN ANCIENT ROME APPLAUSE WAS USED AS A TACTIC FOR INTIMIDATION IN BATTLE OR FOR GAUGING LEADERS' POLITICAL POPULARITY, LIKE A MODERN-DAY POLL.

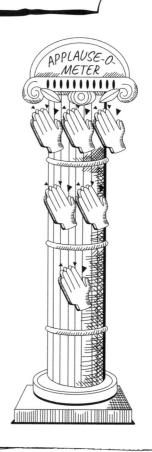

IN 1850s FRANCE IT WAS COMMON PRACTICE TO PAY PEOPLE TO APPLAUD AND BOLSTER AN AUDIENCE'S ENTHUSIASM. THERE WAS EVEN AN AGENCY IN FRANCE FOR HIRING **CLAQUERS**, AS THEY WERE KNOWN. THERE WERE SPECIFIC ROLES WITHIN THE CLAQUE: THE COMMISSAIRES (OFFICERS) TO CALL ATTENTION TO A PIECE'S BEST QUALITIES, THE RIEURS (LAUGHERS), THE CHATOUILLEURS (TICKLERS) TO KEEP THE CROWD IN GOOD SPIRITS, THE PLEUREURS (CRIERS), AND THE BISSEURS (ENCORE-ERS) TO CALL FOR ENCORES.

THIS PRACTICE HAS REMAINED, ONLY NOW AUDIENCES FOLLOW APPLAUSE SIGNALS ON TELEVISION AND LIVE SEGMENTS, OR A LAUGH TRACK IS PLAYED. OUR SYSTEM OF **LIKES** ON SOCIAL MEDIA IS ANOTHER CONTEMPORARY ITERATION OF APPLAUSE; A SEMI-ANONYMOUS FORM OF SUPPORT, BUT WITH A PERSONAL TOUCH NOW THAT OUR PROFILES ARE ATTACHED.

- THE TRADITION OF -

KISSING

LOCKING LIPS

EXPERTS BELIEVE KISSING EVOLVED FROM SNIFFING: ONE OF THE EARLIEST KNOWN DESCRIPTIONS OF KISSING IN VEDIC SANSKRIT TEXTS FROM 1500 BC USE A WORD MEANING SMELL OR SNIFF. HINDU EPIC POEM THE MAHABHARATA CONTAINS THE FIRST WRITTEN ROMANTIC KISS, DESCRIBED AS "SHE SET HER MOUTH TO MY MOUTH."

NEW ARRIVAL!

KISSING APPEARS IN THE OLD TESTAMENT, IN HOMER'S EPICS, AND WAS PROMINENT IN ANCIENT ROMAN SOCIETY AND ART. ACROSS MANY CULTURES AND TIMES, ITS PURPOSE RANGES ANYWHERE FROM AN EXPRESSION OF ROMANCE TO AN INDICATION OF **SOCIAL STANDING**.

BUT IT SEEMS ROMANTIC KISSING IS LESS UBIQUITOUS THAN ONE MIGHT THINK: A 2015 RESEARCH REPORT PUBLISHED IN AMERICAN ANTHROPOLOGIST FOUND THAT **ONLY 46 PERCENT OF CULTURES** ENGAGED IN KISSING OF A ROMANTIC-SEXUAL NATURE.

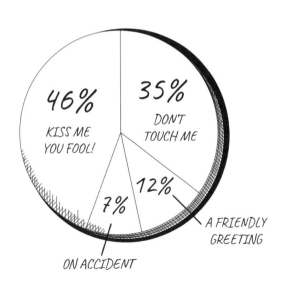

46% KISS ME YOU FOOL!

35% DON'T TOUCH ME

7% ON ACCIDENT

12% A FRIENDLY GREETING

LET US OUT!

IT'S COMMON SENSE TO COVER OUR MOUTHS WHEN WE SNEEZE OR COUGH. THESE TWO OFTEN ACCOMPANY SICKNESS, AND COURTESY TELLS US THAT IT'S POLITE TO SHIELD OTHERS FROM BEING SPRAYED WITH OUR GERMS.

IT TURNS OUT THAT COVERING OUR MOUTHS WHEN WE YAWN COULD COME FROM TRYING TO PROTECT THE YAWNER, INSTEAD: THERE'S AN OLD SUPERSTITION

DATING BACK TO ANCIENT TIMES THAT OPENING THE MOUTH WIDE TO YAWN COULD ALLOW **DEMONS** OR **EVIL SPIRITS** TO ENTER THE BODY.

THERE ARE ALSO ACCOUNTS OF MAKING THE SIGN OF THE CROSS OVER ONE'S YAWN DURING TIMES OF PLAGUE, FEARING THAT YAWNING COULD SPREAD ILLNESS. NOWADAYS, COVERING YAWNS IS CONSIDERED POLITE BECAUSE MANY BELIEVE THAT YAWNING IS A SIGN OF BOREDOM OR DISINTEREST, WHEN ***IT'S MORE LIKELY THE BODY'S WAY OF INTAKING AIR TO COOL THE BRAIN.***

- THE TRADITION OF -
KNOCKING ON WOOD

DON'T JINX YOURSELF

MANY BELIEVE THE TRADITION OF KNOCKING ON WOOD TO AVOID JINXING YOURSELF COMES FROM ANCIENT PAGAN CULTURES' BELIEFS THAT GODS AND SPIRITS LIVED INSIDE TREES. BY RAPPING ON THE TRUNK THEY COULD HAVE CALLED ON GOOD SPIRITS FOR PROTECTION, THANKED THEM FOR GOOD LUCK, OR EVEN WARDED OFF ANY EVIL SPIRITS FROM LISTENING.

HOWEVER, A CHILDREN'S GAME MAY ALSO BE THE SOURCE OF THE RITUAL; A VERSION OF TAG CALLED **TIGGY TOUCHWOOD** WAS PLAYED BY CHILDREN DURING THE 1800s. BY TOUCHING WOOD DURING THE CHASE, THEY COULD BE SAFE FROM BEING TAGGED.

THE PAGAN RITUAL COULD HAVE ALSO BEEN ADAPTED BY CHRISTIANITY. MANY ASSOCIATE WOOD WITH THE CROSS ON WHICH JESUS WAS CRUCIFIED, AND FEEL THAT KNOCKING ON WOOD COULD **BRING OUT THE PROTECTION OF GOD.**

POURING ONE OUT

FOR THE HOMIES

POURING ONE OUT OF YOUR (USUALLY ALCOHOLIC) DRINK ONTO THE
GROUND AS A TRIBUTE TO A FRIEND WHO'S PASSED COMES FROM
MAKING A LIBATION. A LIBATION IS A RITUAL AND OFFERING TO
THE DEAD THAT'S BEEN AROUND SINCE ANCIENT TIMES.

ONE OF THE OLDEST RECORDS OF MAKING LIBATIONS IS FROM **ANCIENT EGYPT.** THEY TYPICALLY POURED OUT WATER FOR THEIR DEAD, SINCE IT GIVES LIFE, BUT THEY ALSO SOMETIMES POURED OUT OTHER LIQUIDS LIKE MILK, HONEY, AND WINE.

POURING OUT ALCOHOL WAS VERY COMMON IN ANCIENT GREECE AS A TRIBUTE TO THE GODS, HEROES, AND THE DEAD, WITH **SPONDAI** BEING A PARTIAL POUR AND **CHOAI** EMPTYING THE LIQUID COMPLETELY. LIBATIONS, WHICH ARE ALSO MENTIONED IN THE BIBLE, WERE CUSTOMARY IN CHINA, AND WERE MADE THROUGHOUT MANY CULTURES. POURING ONE OUT IS ONE OF THE OLDEST EVERYDAY RITUALS.

- THE TRADITION OF -

USING NAPKINS

BETTER THAN YOUR SLEEVE

ONE OF THE EARLIEST USES OF NAPKINS WAS IN ANCIENT GREECE, WHEN SPARTANS USED SMALL PIECES OF DOUGH OR BREAD TO CLEAN THEIR HANDS DURING MEALS. THE ROMANS USED TWO KINDS OF CLOTH NAPKINS CALLED THE *SUDARIUM* AND THE *MAPPA*.

THE SUDARIUM WAS SMALL AND SIMILAR TO A **HANDKERCHIEF** AND WAS USED FOR CLEANING UP DURING MEALS AND WIPING AWAY SWEAT. THE MAPPA WAS TYPICALLY A LARGER THROW

CLOTH THAT **COVERED COUCHES OR CHAIRS** AT MEALTIME. GUESTS OFTEN BROUGHT THEIR OWN MAPPAS AND USED THEM TO WRAP LEFTOVERS AFTER DINING.

CHINA WAS ONE OF THE FIRST PLACES TO USE PAPER NAPKINS WHEN PAPER WAS INVENTED AROUND THE SECOND CENTURY AD. IN EUROPE DURING THE MIDDLE AGES, DINERS USED

THEIR CLOTHING OR BREAD, AND THEN PROGRESSED TO **LARGE COMMUNAL CLOTHS** LAID OVER THE TABLE. THESE EVENTUALLY GAVE WAY TO SMALLER, PERSONAL NAPKINS.

BRUSHING YOUR TEETH TWICE A DAY

DO IT FOR YOUR DENTIST

MANY ANCIENT CIVILIZATIONS USED FRAYED TWIGS FROM CLEANSING OR AROMATIC TREES AS CHEW STICKS TO CLEAN THEIR TEETH. RAGS AND A VARIETY OF POWDERS, ROOTS, AND OILS WERE ALSO POPULAR BEFORE TOOTHBRUSHES WERE INVENTED.

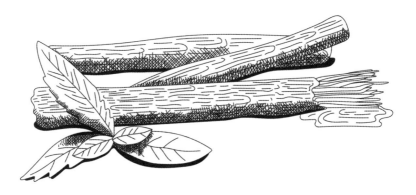

WE DON'T KNOW THE EXACT TIME WHEN BRUSHING TEETH BECAME A DAILY PRACTICE, BUT THERE IS MENTION OF **THE PROPHET MUHAMMAD** CLEANING HIS TEETH MULTIPLE TIMES A DAY IN MANY NARRATIONS OF ISLAM. HE USED MISWAK, A TWIG FROM THE **SALVADORA PERSICA** TREE, KNOWN FOR ITS TEETH-CLEANING BENEFITS.

SALVADORA PERSICA
BRUSHETHA YOURICA TEETHIS

IN THE UNITED STATES, DAILY TOOTH BRUSHING BECAME MORE POPULAR AFTER **WORLD WAR II.** THE SOLDIERS HAD HYGIENE REQUIREMENTS THAT REQUIRED THEM TO BRUSH THEIR TEETH REGULARLY, AND THEY BROUGHT THE ROUTINE HOME WITH THEM AFTER THE WAR.

GIVING A THUMBS UP

GOOD TO GO

IT IS WIDELY BELIEVED THAT THE THUMBS UP GESTURE CAME FROM GLADIATOR BATTLES IN ANCIENT ROME: THAT WHEN A GLADIATOR WAS TO BE SPARED, THE SPECTATORS SIGNALED A THUMBS UP, AND WHEN HE WAS TO BE KILLED, A THUMBS DOWN.

IT TURNS OUT THAT THIS IS A MISCONCEPTION DUE TO TRANSLATION, AND IT IS LIKELY THAT **AN EXTENDED THUMB SIGNALED TO KILL, AND A CONCEALED OR TUCKED THUMB MEANT TO SPARE.** IN REALITY, THE ORIGIN OF THE THUMBS UP MEANING OK LIKELY CAME FROM NORTHERN EUROPE.

CAN'T WE ALL JUST GET ALONG?

IN FACT, WHEN SURVEYED BY ANTHROPOLOGIST DESMOND MORRIS, MANY ITALIANS WERE SURPRISED TO HEAR THAT THE GESTURE WAS THOUGHT TO ORIGINATE IN ROME. THEY RECOGNIZED IT AS A GESTURE BROUGHT OVER BY **AMERICAN GIs** DURING WORLD WAR II AS A READY SIGNAL USED BY FIGHTER PILOTS.

- THE TRADITION OF -

SAYING HELLO AND GOODBYE

COMING AND GOING

IT TURNS OUT THAT THE GREETING HELLO IS A FAIRLY NEW ONE: IT DATES BACK TO THE EARLY 1800s, WHERE IT WAS MAINLY AN EXPRESSION OF SURPRISE OR A CALL FOR ATTENTION. IT WAS THOMAS EDISON WHO FIRST USED THE WORD AS A GREETING WHEN ANSWERING THE TELEPHONE.

HELLO?!

THE INVENTOR OF THE TELEPHONE, ALEXANDER GRAHAM BELL, RIVALED EDISON'S CHOICE AND INSISTED ON **AHOY** AS THE PROPER CHOICE, BUT EDISON'S WON OUT. THE FIRST OPERATING MANUALS SUGGESTED EITHER HELLO OR WHAT IS WANTED, AND THE QUICKER OPTION STUCK.

GOODBYE, ON THE OTHER HAND, COMES FROM THE ORIGINAL PHRASE **GOD BE WITH YE.** THE CONTRACTION GODBWYE OF THE PHRASE APPEARED SOMETIME DURING THE LATE 1500s AND IS THOUGHT TO HAVE BEEN INFLUENCED BY PARTING PHRASES LIKE GOOD DAY AND GOOD NIGHT TO EVENTUALLY BECOME GOODBYE.

- THE TRADITION OF -

TAKING YOUR SHOES OFF AT HOME

KEEPING OUTSIDE OUTSIDE

REMOVING ONE'S SHOES UPON ENTERING THE HOME IS A REGULAR PRACTICE IN MANY COUNTRIES. WHILE THERE IS NO RECORD OF ITS PRECISE ORIGIN, THE CUSTOM SEEMS TO HAVE BEEN MOST COMMON IN AREAS THROUGHOUT ASIA AND THE MIDDLE EAST AS AN ACT OF CLEANLINESS AND RESPECT.

FROM **JAPAN** TO **THAILAND,** MANY ACTIVITIES IN TRADITIONAL HOMES OFTEN INVOLVE SPENDING A LOT OF TIME ON THE FLOOR SITTING, EATING, AND EVEN SLEEPING, SO REMOVING ONES' SHOES FOR CLEANLINESS MAKES SENSE.

MEMBERS OF THE **MUSLIM FAITH** REMOVE SHOES BEFORE PRAYING, AND IT IS CUSTOMARY TO REMOVE SHOES BEFORE ENTERING TEMPLES AND HOUSES OF WORSHIP ACROSS MANY RELIGIONS AS A SIGN OF RESPECT. IT LIKELY CAUGHT ON IN SO MANY CULTURES TODAY BECAUSE NO ONE WANTS MUD AND DIRT TRACKED INTO THE HOUSE.

- THE TRADITION OF -

GOING TO PROM

A NIGHT YOU'LL NEVER FORGET

FORMAL DANCES AND BALLS TAKE PLACE IN COUNTRIES ACROSS THE WORLD, AND IN THE UNITED STATES, PROM IS ONE OF THE BIGGEST CULTURAL RITES OF PASSAGE FOR YOUNG PEOPLE. THE EARLIEST REFERENCES TO PROM, SHORT FOR *PROMENADE,* COME FROM THE LATE 1800s, AS A COED DANCE BETWEEN COLLEGES THAT WERE SPLIT BY GENDER.

THE TRADITION LIKELY COMBINED WITH THE INSTITUTION OF **DEBUTANTE BALLS**, A DEBUT FOR YOUNG, WEALTHY WOMEN INTO MARRIAGE AND SOCIETY. BY THE 1920s PROM REPRESENTED THE DEBUT OF TEENS INTO ADULTHOOD, BECOMING MOST POPULAR IN THE '50s. LIKE SCHOOLS AT THE TIME, EARLY PROMS WERE SEGREGATED AND EXCLUDED BLACK STUDENTS.

EVEN AFTER INTEGRATION, MANY SCHOOLS IN THE 1960s AND '70s HELD **SEPARATE PROMS** FOR THEIR WHITE AND BLACK STUDENTS. PROM BECAME SO IMPORTANT TO TEENAGERS THAT THERE IS EVEN RECORD OF CHICAGO PRINCIPALS **CANCELLING THEIR PROMS DURING THE GREAT DEPRESSION** OUT OF SENSITIVITY TO STUDENTS WHO COULDN'T AFFORD TO GO. TO THIS DAY, PROM REPRESENTS AN IMPORTANT **COMING-OF-AGE RITUAL** FOR HIGH SCHOOLERS ACROSS THE UNITED STATES.

PROM
POPULARITY RULES OVER MAJORITY

- THE TRADITION OF -

THE HIGH FIVE

GIMME SOME SKIN

THE HIGH FIVE HAS ITS ORIGIN IN AFRICAN AMERICAN CULTURE FROM AROUND THE TIME OF WORLD WAR II. IT LIKELY GREW AS A VARIATION OF HANDSHAKES AND GESTURES LIKE THE LOW FIVE OR "GIMME SOME SKIN."

THE EXACT MOMENT THESE TRANSITIONED TO THE HIGH FIVE IS UNKNOWN, BUT MOST SPECULATE IT CAME ALONG IN **THE SPORTS WORLD.** RUMORS OF THE FIRST HIGH FIVE RANGE FROM ONE FAMOUSLY EXCHANGED BETWEEN DUSTY BAKER AND GLENN BURKE AT A DODGERS GAME IN 1977, TO THE WORLD OF WOMEN'S VOLLEYBALL IN THE 1960s.

HOWEVER, THERE IS A HIGH FIVE FEATURED IN A SCENE FROM JEAN-LUC GODARD'S 1960 FRENCH FILM **BREATHLESS,** SHOWING THAT THE TRUTH OF THE FIRST HIGH FIVE WILL REMAIN A MYSTERY.

- THE TRADITION OF -

WEARING WHITE TO YOUR WEDDING

SOMETHING BORROWED, SOMETHING BLUE

IN MANY CULTURES WHITE IS NOT THE CUSTOMARY COLOR FOR WEDDING DRESSES, AND IT TURNS OUT THAT THE TREND WASN'T ALWAYS A STAPLE OF WESTERN CULTURE EITHER. BEFORE AND DURING THE VICTORIAN ERA, IT WAS COMMON FOR EUROPEAN BRIDES TO WEAR A VARIETY OF COLORS AND EMBELLISHMENTS ON THEIR WEDDING DAYS.

I'M WEARING BLACK TO MATCH MY SOUL.

THOUGH BRIDES HAD WORN WHITE BEFORE, **QUEEN VICTORIA'S** CHOICE TO WEAR A WHITE DRESS FOR HER WEDDING TO PRINCE ALBERT IN 1840 SET THE PRECEDENT FOR WHITE AS THE POPULAR CHOICE.

THE WHITE WEDDING DRESS CAUGHT ON BECAUSE IT SYMBOLIZED **PURITY AND INNOCENCE,** BUT ALSO BECAUSE IT WAS A SUBTLE **SHOW OF WEALTH.** BECAUSE IT'S SO EASY TO STAIN AND HARD TO CLEAN, WEARING THE COLOR SHOWED THAT THE BRIDE COULD AFFORD THE FRIVOLITY OF CHOOSING WHITE.

BLESSING A SNEEZE

IN CASE YOUR HEART STOPS

SAYING "BLESS YOU" IN RESPONSE TO A SNEEZE *IS SAID TO COME FROM THE PLAGUE AROUND 590 AD, WHEN POPE GREGORY I SUPPOSEDLY DECREED TO OFFER GOD'S BLESSING WHEN SOMEONE SNEEZED, AS IT COULD BE A SYMPTOM OF THE PLAGUE.*

OH BOY, YOU'RE PROBABLY GOING TO DIE.

STILL OTHERS BELIEVE THAT IN ANCIENT TIMES, SNEEZING WAS THOUGHT TO BE A WAY OF **EXPELLING EVIL SPIRITS FROM THE BODY,** SO A BLESSING WAS OFFERED AS PROTECTION.

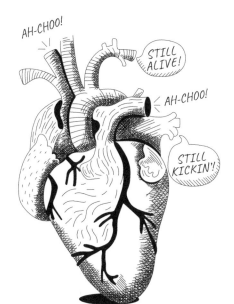

THERE IS ALSO THE THEORY THAT "BLESS YOU" WAS SAID BECAUSE OF THE **SUPERSTITION** THAT THE HEART STOPS DURING A SNEEZE, WHICH WE NOW KNOW TO BE UNTRUE.

- THE TRADITION OF -

NOT POINTING AT OTHERS

KEEP YOUR FINGERS TO YOURSELF

THOUGH THERE IS NO SOLID EVIDENCE TO EXPLAIN WHY, POINTING DIRECTLY AT OTHER PEOPLE IS CONSIDERED RUDE IN MANY COUNTRIES. SOME DICTIONARY DEFINITIONS OF FINGER-POINTING DESCRIBE IT AS A METHOD OF ACCUSATION AND USE IT AS AN EXAMPLE OF RUDE BEHAVIOR.

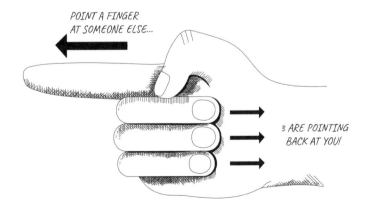

POINT A FINGER AT SOMEONE ELSE...

3 ARE POINTING BACK AT YOU!

THERE IS A RUMOR THAT THE RULE IS DUE TO OLD IDEAS OF **POINTING BEING USED TO PERFORM A HEX,** THOUGH THERE IS NO CONCRETE PROOF ON THE MATTER. IT IS MORE LIKELY THAT THE PHYSICAL NATURE OF THE GESTURE FEELS DIRECT AND AGGRESSIVE, AND CALLS ATTENTION TO THE RECIPIENT.

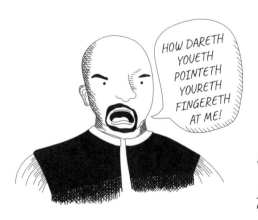

HOW DARETH YOUETH POINTETH YOURETH FINGERETH AT ME!

THERE IS EVEN MENTION OF POINTING AS A NEGATIVE ACT DATING BACK TO SHAKESPEARE'S WORK. IN ACT 4, SCENE 2 OF OTHELLO, **OTHELLO LAMENTS THAT GOD IS POINTING AT HIM AS A FOOL:** "BUT, ALAS, TO MAKE ME / THE FIXED FIGURE FOR THE TIME OF SCORN / TO POINT HIS SLOW AND MOVING FINGER AT!"

- THE TRADITION OF -

RUNNING MARATHONS

GOING THE DISTANCE

LEGEND HAS IT THAT MARATHONS COME FROM THE GREEK MESSENGER *PHEIDIPPIDES,* WHO IN 490 BC RAN ABOUT 25 MILES FROM MARATHON TO ATHENS TO DELIVER NEWS OF VICTORY AGAINST THE PERSIAN ARMY, AND DROPPED DEAD ON ARRIVAL.

MARATHONS AT THE FIRST MODERN OLYMPIC GAMES IN 1896 MIRRORED PHEIDIPPIDES' DISTANCE, AND IT WASN'T UNTIL THE 1908 GAMES IN LONDON THAT THE NOW-STANDARD 26.2-MILE LENGTH CAME TO BE. IT'S SAID THAT **THE ROYAL FAMILY** WANTED THE RACE TO START AT WINDSOR CASTLE SO THE CHILDREN COULD SEE IT FROM THEIR NURSERY, AND THEY WANTED IT TO END IN FRONT OF THEIR ROYAL BOX AT THE WHITE CITY STADIUM.

MAKE IT LONGER AT ONCE!

THE EXTRA 1.2 MILES WERE ADDED, AND BY 1921 26.2 MILES WAS THE STANDARD LENGTH. THE DRAMATIC FINISH OF THE 1908 MARATHON'S WINNER, AN UNDERDOG NAMED DORANDO PIETRI, MAY HAVE POPULARIZED 26.2 MILES AS THE ULTIMATE BREAKING POINT FOR RUNNERS. **SHERLOCK HOLMES AUTHOR SIR ARTHUR CONAN DOYLE** WROTE ABOUT HOW PIETRI COLLAPSED AS HE NEARED THE FINISH LINE AND WAS DRAGGED ACROSS WITH THE HELP OF CHEERING OFFICIALS.

- THE TRADITION OF -

FLOSSING TEETH

A FAVOR FOR YOUR GUMS

THE EARLIEST CREDIT FOR FLOSSING GOES TO LEVI SPEAR PARMLY, A NEW ORLEANS DENTIST WHO PROPOSED FLOSSING TEETH IN HIS 1819 BOOK A PRACTICAL GUIDE TO THE MANAGEMENT OF THE TEETH. HE DESCRIBES USING A WAXED SILKEN THREAD TO REMOVE FOOD FROM THE TEETH AND GUMS.

BY THE LATE 1800s **DENTAL FLOSS** WAS COMMERCIALLY PRODUCED, AND ADVANCED WITH THE EMERGENCE OF NYLON AS AN ALTERNATIVE TO SILK. FLOSS WAS MADE WAXED, FLAVORED, AND IN A VARIETY OF DISPENSERS FROM TIN TO GLASS TO WOOD.

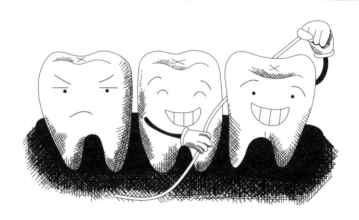

FLOSSING HAS BEEN SAID TO BE VITAL TO DENTAL HEALTH FOR YEARS SINCE, BUT RECENT RESEARCH IN 2011 FOUND THAT WHILE FLOSSING CAN HELP REDUCE RISK OF **GINGIVITIS**, THERE'S NOT MUCH EVIDENCE TO SHOW THAT IT SIGNIFICANTLY FIGHTS PLAQUE.

- THE TRADITION OF -
COMPOSTING
FROM OLD GROWS NEW

EVIDENCE FROM EARLY CIVILIZATIONS IN SCOTLAND, GREECE, ROME, AND CHINA SUGGESTS COMPOSTING. INDIGENOUS AMERICANS HAD MANY SOPHISTICATED METHODS OF COMPOSTING, AND PLANTED SEEDS WITH FISH PARTS TO STRENGTHEN GROWTH.

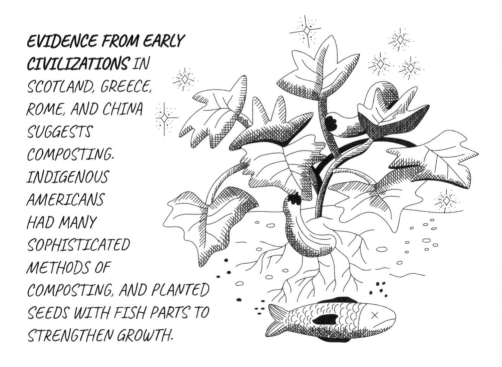

GEORGE WASHINGTON HAD A **STERCORARY** AT MOUNT VERNON TO HOLD MANURE AND WASTE FOR COMPOST. SIR ALBERT HOWARD, NOTED FOR HIS WORK IN ORGANIC FARMING, DEVELOPED THE INDORE PROCESS IN THE EARLY 1900s IN INDIA. HIS METHOD FEATURED LAYER-BASED COMPOSTING.

AS SUSTAINABILITY AND WASTE HAVE TAKEN UP MORE SPACE IN THE GLOBAL CONVERSATION, PRACTICES ARE CHANGING. IN **SOUTH KOREA, 95 PERCENT OF FOOD WASTE IS RECYCLED** AFTER A PUSH FOR BETTER WASTE MANAGEMENT FOLLOWING THE COUNTRY'S INDUSTRIALIZATION IN THE 1990s. BINS THAT CHARGE FOR WASTE BY WEIGHT HAVE HELPED INCENTIVIZE MORE CONSCIOUS HABITS.

- THE TRADITION OF -

GIVING TWO WEEKS' NOTICE

I REGRET TO INFORM YOU...

2 WEEKS' NOTICE

GIVING A FORTNIGHT'S NOTICE WHEN LEAVING A JOB HAS BEEN UNDERSTOOD AS THE STANDARD WHEN IT COMES TO WORKPLACE ETIQUETTE IN THE UNITED STATES. THE IDEA BEHIND THE RULE IS THAT GIVING TWO WEEKS' NOTICE ALLOWS AN EMPLOYER ENOUGH TIME TO INTERVIEW AND TRAIN A REPLACEMENT FOR THE POSITION.

BUT CONVERSATIONS ABOUT **MUTUAL WORKPLACE RESPECT** AND **EQUITY** CALL THE PRACTICE INTO QUESTION. WHILE IT'S TAUGHT THAT GIVING TWO WEEKS' NOTICE IS VITAL TO MAINTAIN A GOOD REPUTATION IN YOUR INDUSTRY, MOST EMPLOYERS GIVE NO NOTICE WHEN DISMISSING A WORKER, AND ARE LIKELY TO FIRE YOU ON THE SPOT.

NO VAST DATA IS AVAILABLE ON THE TREND YET, BUT SOME ECONOMISTS AND RECRUITERS CLAIM THAT **FEWER AND FEWER** PEOPLE FOLLOW THE OLD TWO WEEKS' NOTICE RULE AND ARE LEAVING JOBS WITHOUT A WARNING. THIS COULD BE DUE TO JOB COMPETITION, UNEMPLOYMENT RATES, OR A CHANGE IN ATTITUDE WITH THE FAST-PACED WORLD OF SOCIAL MEDIA AND TECHNOLOGY.

LEAVING A PARTY WITHOUT SAYING GOODBYE

IT'S EASIER THIS WAY

S.S. BUH-BYE

THE NOTION OF LEAVING A PARTY WITHOUT SAYING GOODBYE IS OFTEN CALLED AN IRISH GOODBYE. *IT'S ATTRIBUTED TO THE DEPARTURE OF MANY OF THE IRISH DURING THE GREAT FAMINE THAT BEGAN IN 1845, IMPLYING THAT FAREWELLS WERE SKIPPED TO AVOID SADNESS. IN REALITY, THIS RUMOR IS UNFOUNDED.*

A SUPPOSED FRENCH CUSTOM FROM THE EIGHTEENTH CENTURY INVOLVES LEAVING WITHOUT SAYING GOODBYE TO AVOID INTERRUPTING THE HOST, BUT APPARENTLY

THE FRENCH IN TURN ASSOCIATED THE HABIT WITH THE ENGLISH, SHOWING THAT IT'S MOST LIKELY A CASE OF **RIVALRY-BASED RUMORS.**

THE TERM **FRENCH LEAVE** APPEARS THROUGHOUT THE 1800s AND 1900s AS A DESCRIPTION OF MILITARY LEAVE IN PUBLICATIONS AND MEMOIRS, SHOWING THE ASSOCIATION COULD HAVE BEEN BORN FROM PREJUDICE AFTER A HISTORY OF WAR.

- THE TRADITION OF -
WEARING DEODORANT

A PUBLIC SERVICE

BEFORE MODERN DEODORANT WAS INVENTED, PEOPLE MADE CREATIVE EFFORTS TO MASK THE STENCH OF BODY ODOR. PERFUMES WERE VERY POPULAR AMONG ANCIENT EGYPTIANS, FOR EXAMPLE, WHO ALSO MADE PASTES, MIXTURES, AND OILS WORN TO COMBAT THE SMELL. THEY EVEN WORE JEWELRY DESIGNED TO CARRY PLEASANT SCENTS.

IN **VICTORIAN SOCIETY,** THE NORM WAS TO TRY AND KEEP ONESELF CLEAN AND MASK ANYTHING ELSE WITH PERFUME. PEOPLE WORE CLOTH PADS AS UNDERARM LINERS, AND WOMEN HAD DRESS SHIELDS TO PROTECT THEIR DRESSES FROM UNDERARM SWEAT.

THE FIRST DEODORANT CALLED **MUM** WAS INVENTED IN 1888, AND BY THE MID-1900s, THE USE OF DEODORANT ROSE BY FIRST PANDERING TO THE INSECURITIES OF WOMEN'S BODY ODOR, AND THEN INCLUDING MEN.

NOT TALKING ON THE PHONE IN PUBLIC

KEEP YOUR CONVO TO YOURSELF

YEAH! YOU DID THAT?! NO WAY MAN, OF COURSE! STEAKS, YES!

WE'VE ALL BEEN ON A BUS OR CROWDED TRAIN AND HEARD SOMEONE HAVING A LOUD PHONE CONVERSATION THAT DISRUPTS THE PEACE. A 2010 CORNELL UNIVERSITY STUDY FOUND THAT OVERHEARING ONLY HALF OF A CONVERSATION FROM SOMEONE TALKING ON THE PHONE IS ACTUALLY MORE DISTRACTING BECAUSE OUR BRAINS ATTEMPT TO FILL THE GAPS. THIS COULD EXPLAIN WHY HEARING ONE SIDE OF A PHONE CALL FEELS ESPECIALLY ANNOYING.

WHEN SURVEYED BY PEW RESEARCH IN 2015, AROUND THREE-QUARTERS OF ADULTS SAID IT'S OK TO USE CELLPHONES WHILE WALKING DOWN THE STREET, ON PUBLIC TRANSPORTATION, AND WHILE WAITING IN LINE. APPROVAL OF PHONE USE IN PUBLIC SEEMED TO GO DOWN THE MORE **INTIMATE** A PUBLIC SETTING WAS.

PHONE USE ACCEPTANCE

ON THE STREET | WAITING IN LINE | RIDING ON A BUS | IN A RESTAURANT, ON A DATE, WITH <u>ME</u>

SLIDE TO POWER OFF

DID YOU EVER CONSIDER ME NEEDING A BREAK FROM YOU?

THIRTY-EIGHT PERCENT SURVEYED SAID CELLPHONE USE IS ACCEPTABLE IN A RESTAURANT, 12 PERCENT SAID IT'S OK AT A FAMILY DINNER, AND ONLY 5 PERCENT OR LESS APPROVED DURING A MEETING, AT A MOVIE THEATER, AND AT CHURCH OR A WORSHIP SERVICE. OVERALL, IT'S CLEAR THAT FOR PERSONAL INTERACTIONS AND QUIET EVENTS, IT'S BEST TO **PUT THE PHONE AWAY.**

GHOSTING

MANY OF US ARE GUILTY OF GHOSTING WHEN WE WANT TO END A RELATIONSHIP WITHOUT GIVING AN UNCOMFORTABLE EXPLANATION. PEOPLE HAVE ALWAYS AVOIDED RETURNING LETTERS OR CALLS FROM UNWANTED SUITORS, BUT SOCIAL MEDIA HAS MADE GHOSTING A PHENOMENON. IT'S EASY AS A GHOSTER TO IGNORE A MESSAGE OR HIT BLOCK, AND YET UNCOMFORTABLE BECAUSE YOU KNOW THE PERSON WILL EVENTUALLY REALIZE YOU'RE AVOIDING THEM.

THE TERM DEVELOPED IN THE EARLY 2000s, WITH THE SURGE OF TECHNOLOGY AND SOCIAL MEDIA. THE FACT THAT SO MUCH INITIAL DATING AND FLIRTATION TAKES PLACE ON APPS LOWERS THE STAKES. WHEN YOU'RE MESSAGING A WIDE POOL OF PEOPLE ON A DATING APP, THE **IMPERSONAL NATURE** AND SHEER VOLUME OF CHOICES OFTEN MAKES GHOSTING THE MOST EFFICIENT OPTION.

PEOPLE GHOST FOR DIFFERENT REASONS, BUT A COMMON THREAD AMONG **SELF-ADMITTED GHOSTERS** IS THE DESIRE TO AVOID CONFLICT OR THE DIFFICULT CONVERSATION OF REJECTING SOMEONE. WHATEVER THE REASON, IF YOU DON'T WANT TO TALK TO SOMEONE ANYMORE, SIMPLY NEVER ANSWERING THEIR TEXTS CAN BE THE EASY WAY OUT.

- THE TRADITION OF -
BRIDAL SHOWERS
IT'S RAINING GIFTS

BRIDAL SHOWERS ARE SAID TO HAIL BACK TO SIXTEENTH CENTURY HOLLAND. *A BRIDE TYPICALLY RECEIVED GIFTS FROM FRIENDS IN PLACE OF A DOWRY IF HER FAMILY WAS TOO POOR TO GIVE ONE, OR HER FATHER DID NOT APPROVE OF THE MARRIAGE.*

THERE IS A DUTCH TALE ABOUT A GIRL WHO FELL IN LOVE WITH A POOR MAN, AND HER FATHER REFUSED TO PROVIDE HER DOWRY UNLESS SHE MARRIED SOMEONE WEALTHY. HER FRIENDS AND NEIGHBORS DECIDED TO SHOWER HER WITH GIFTS TO COMPENSATE AND, WARMED BY THE GESTURE, HER FATHER APPROVED OF THE UNION.

THIS CHEST IS FULL OF HOPE FOR DEEP AND ETERNAL LOVE...SIGHHH.....

IN THE VICTORIAN ERA, BRIDES WERE GIVEN A **TROUSSEAU** OF ITEMS AND HOUSEHOLD GOODS, OFTEN SAVED YEARS IN ADVANCE IN A **HOPE CHEST**. BRIDAL SHOWERS TODAY ARE OFTEN OPPORTUNITIES TO CELEBRATE WITH A PARTY AND STILL SERVE THE PURPOSE OF GATHERING USEFUL GIFTS FOR THE BRIDE.

- THE TRADITION OF -

SENDING AN RSVP

WITH OR WITHOUT REGRETS

REPONDEZ
S'IL VOUS
PLAIT!

RSVP HAS BECOME THE MODERN STANDARD FOR ALMOST ALL FORMAL INVITATIONS. THE ABBREVIATION COMES FROM THE FRENCH PHRASE REPONDEZ S'IL VOUS PLAIT, OR "RESPOND IF YOU PLEASE."

THE PHRASE BECAME POPULAR ON ENGLISH INVITATIONS AROUND THE 1800s AS A FASHIONABLE OPTION AMONG HIGH SOCIETY. A BOOK ON SOCIAL ETIQUETTE FROM 1878 CLAIMED THAT RSVP WAS **GOING OUT OF FASHION**. TURNS OUT THEY WERE WRONG!

THE ABBREVIATION HAS TAKEN ON A LIFE OF ITS OWN, AND IS OFTEN USED MORE INFORMALLY: IN ENGLISH, IT HAS BECOME COMMON TO USE RSVP AS **A VERB,** OR TO WRITE, REDUNDANTLY, "PLEASE RSVP." ONCE RESERVED FOR FORMAL OCCASIONS OR WEDDINGS, NOWADAYS YOU CAN USUALLY SEND YOUR RESPONSE VIA EMAIL OR TEXT WITH NO CONCERN OF OFFENDING THE ELITE.

- THE TRADITION OF -
KEEPING YOUR ELBOWS OFF THE TABLE
NO ELBOWS FOR DINNER

MOST OF US HAVE HEARD SINCE CHILDHOOD THAT IT IS RUDE TO PUT YOUR ELBOWS ON THE TABLE DURING A MEAL. SOME SAY THIS COMES FROM MEDIEVAL TIMES WHEN SPACE WAS SCARCE AT LONG, CROWDED TABLES DURING FEASTS.

STILL, OTHERS THEORIZE THAT HAVING ELBOWS ON THE TABLE ENCOURAGED **SLOUCHING** OR INDICATED TOO COMFORTABLE AND INFORMAL AN ATTITUDE FOR DINNER. ANOTHER IDEA CLAIMS THAT HAVING ELBOWS ON THE TABLE MADE YOU **LOOK TOO EAGER TO EAT**.

THERE ARE EVEN TALES THAT **SAILORS USED THEIR ELBOWS TO STEADY THEIR PLATES ON THE WATER**, OR THAT THE POSITION IMPLIES ONE GUARDING THEIR FOOD, BOTH INDICATIONS OF LOWER CLASS. NO SINGLE ORIGIN CAN BE CONFIRMED, AND IT LIKELY COMES FROM A COMBINATION OF THEM ALL.

THE PEACE SIGN

THROWING UP DEUCES

A POPULAR MYTH CLAIMS THAT THE PEACE SIGN COMES FROM THE HUNDRED YEARS WAR IN THE FOURTEENTH AND FIFTEENTH CENTURY, WHEN THE FRENCH CUT OFF THE INDEX AND MIDDLE FINGERS OF ANY CAPTURED ENGLISH ARCHERS TO RUIN THEIR LONGBOW SKILLS.

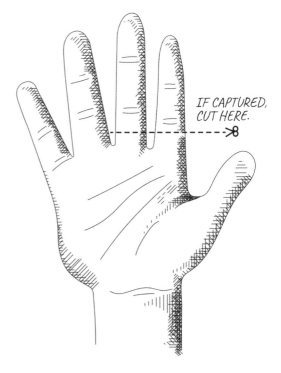

IF CAPTURED, CUT HERE.

THE STORY CLAIMS THE ENGLISH THEN BEGAN TO RAISE THEIR TWO FINGERS AT THE FRENCH TO TAUNT THEM DURING BATTLE, BUT THERE IS NO REAL EVIDENCE OF THIS. THE LONGBOW TYPICALLY REQUIRES THE USE OF THREE FINGERS, AND AN ACCOUNT BY CHRONICLER JEAN DE WAVRIN CLAIMS THAT IT WAS **THREE FINGERS** THEY CUT OFF, NOT TWO.

NOT TO BE A KNOW-IT-ALL, BUT IT WAS ACTUALLY 3.

PEACE, NOT WAR!

IN REALITY, THE TWO-FINGER GESTURE HAS LONG BEEN ONE OF INSULT IN MANY COUNTRIES LIKE THE UNITED KINGDOM, AUSTRALIA, AND NEW ZEALAND. THE **V-SIGN** WAS USED TO REPRESENT VICTORY DURING WORLD WAR II AND WAS THEN CO-OPTED AS A SIGNAL OF PEACE BY THE **ANTI-WAR COUNTERCULTURE** IN THE 1960s.

- THE TRADITION OF -

WEARING BLACK TO A FUNERAL

THE ORIGINAL BAIT-AND-HOOK BUSINESS MODEL

ONE OF THE EARLIEST RECORDS OF WEARING BLACK TO MOURN IS FROM ANCIENT ROME, WHEN PEOPLE WORE THE TOGA PULLA FOR FUNERAL PROCESSIONS. THE TOGA PULLA WAS A TOGA DYED DARK OR FLIPPED TO CONCEAL THE PURPLE BORDER.

I'M SO SAD... BUT SO EXCITED FOR MY OUTFIT POSSIBILITIES

WEARING BLACK WHILE IN MOURNING BECAME QUITE POPULAR DURING **THE VICTORIAN ERA.** IT WAS GENERALLY CUSTOM TO WEAR BLACK FOR ABOUT A YEAR FOLLOWING A DEATH, AFTER WHICH PURPLES AND GREYS IN **HALF MOURNING** COULD BE INTRODUCED AS WELL. THOSE WHO COULD AFFORD TO OWNED SEPARATE WARDROBES SPECIFICALLY FOR MOURNING.

QUEEN VICTORIA HELPED POPULARIZE MOURNING FASHION, AS SHE FAMOUSLY WORE BLACK UNTIL THE END OF HER LIFE AFTER THE DEATH OF HER HUSBAND, PRINCE ALBERT. MOURNING COLORS DIFFER AROUND THE WORLD: **WHITE** IS SOMETIMES WORN IN CHINA, AND AT HINDU FUNERALS.

PINKY SWEARS

CROSS MY HEART AND HOPE TO DIE

WE KNOW THAT PINKY SWEARS HAVE BEEN AROUND SINCE AT LEAST THE 1800s, *AS THE ENTRY FOR PINKY IN THE 1860 DICTIONARY OF AMERICANISMS BY JOHN RUSSELL BARTLETT DESCRIBES CHILDREN INTERLOCKING PINKIES IN ORDER TO MAKE A BARGAIN.*

SOME THEORIZE THAT THE PINKY SWEAR WAS ADAPTED FROM THE JAPANESE VERSION YUBIKIRI, WHICH TRANSLATES TO "FINGER CUTTING." THE IDEA IS THAT IF YOU BREAK THE PROMISE, YOU WILL LOSE YOUR LITTLE FINGER.

YOU HAVE BETRAYED ME!

GOOD LUCK!

DIFFERENT VERSIONS OF AN ACCOMPANYING SONG SAY THAT WHOEVER LIES MUST **CUT OFF THEIR FINGER, RECEIVE A THOUSAND FIST-PUNCHINGS,** AND **SWALLOW A THOUSAND NEEDLES.** IT COULD ALSO COME FROM MEDIEVAL-ERA PROSTITUTES CUTTING OFF THE TIPS OF THEIR LITTLE FINGERS AS DISPLAYS OF DEVOTION, A GESTURE THAT WAS CONSIDERED HONORABLE.

- THE TRADITION OF -
LISTENING TO CHRISTMAS MUSIC

SLEIGH BELLS RING, ARE YOU LISTENING?

LOVE IT OR HATE IT, WHEN WINTERTIME ROLLS AROUND IN THE UNITED STATES YOU'RE SURE TO START HEARING CHRISTMAS MUSIC IN ALMOST ANY SHOP YOU ENTER. THE FIRST CHRISTMAS SONGS WERE WRITTEN AS EARLY AS THE MIDDLE AGES. MOST WERE TRANSLATED AND SOLIDIFIED INTO THE VERSIONS WE RECOGNIZE TODAY DURING THE 1700s-1800s.

I WAS PARDONED! IT IS THE MOST WONDERFUL TIME OF THE YEAR!

NIELSEN'S MUSIC 360 REPORT FOUND THAT THE GENERATION WHO LIKES HOLIDAY MUSIC THE MOST ARE **MILLENNIALS.** THIS IS SURPRISING WHEN YOU CONSIDER THAT MANY OF

I'M...DREAMING OF MY CHILDHOOD CHRISTMAS!

THE POPULAR CHRISTMAS SONGS TODAY WERE RELEASED IN THE 1940s AND '50s. THIRTY-ONE PERCENT OF GEN XERS WERE HOLIDAY MUSIC FANS AFTER MILLENNIALS, AND BOOMERS CAME IN AT ONLY 25 PERCENT.

ME TOO KID... ME TOO.

WHETHER YOU START BLASTING "JINGLE BELL ROCK" ON DECEMBER 1, THE SECOND A CHILL HITS THE AIR, OR ABSOLUTELY NEVER, **RETAIL EMPLOYEES** SEEM LIKELY TO GET SICK OF CHRISTMAS MUSIC MORE THAN THE REST OF US. SOME PSYCHOLOGISTS AND THERAPISTS HAVE POINTED OUT THAT GETTING SUCH A CONSTANT DOSE OF HOLIDAY MUSIC IS BOUND TO IRRITATE SHOPKEEPERS EVENTUALLY.

- THE TRADITION OF -
CLEANING YOUR PLATE

DO YOU WANT SECONDS?

THERE ARE MANY DIFFERENT DINING TRADITIONS IN EVERY CULTURE AROUND THE WORLD. THOUGH THEY MIGHT NOT BE SO STRICT IN PRACTICE ANYMORE, HERE ARE SOME OF THE MOST INTERESTING CUSTOMS AROUND HOW TO TREAT YOUR DISHES.

MEMBER OF THE CLEAN PLATE CLUB

I GET A 10-SECOND HEAD START!

IN CHINA, IT'S CUSTOMARY TO **LEAVE A LITTLE BIT OF FOOD ON THE PLATE** TO SIGNAL YOU'RE FULL, WHEREAS CLEANING YOUR PLATE CAN BE A SIGN YOU HAVE ROOM TO EAT MORE. IN SOUTH KOREA IT'S EXPECTED THAT **THE OLDEST PERSON BEGIN EATING FIRST,** AND THIS SEEMS TO BE A COMMON COURTESY THROUGHOUT MANY AREAS OF EAST ASIA.

IN JAPAN **YOU SHOULDN'T STICK YOUR CHOPSTICKS STRAIGHT UP INTO A BOWL OF RICE,** BECAUSE THAT'S HOW A BOWL OF RICE IS OFFERED TO THE DEAD. IF A MEAL IS SERVED OVER A **BANANA LEAF** IN INDIA, FOLD THE LEAF TOWARDS YOU TO INDICATE SATISFACTION; FOLDING THE LEAF AWAY IS TYPICALLY RESERVED FOR SOLEMN OCCASIONS LIKE FUNERALS.

- THE TRADITION OF -

MOONING

NOT THE ONE IN THE SKY

MOONING HAS BEEN AROUND SINCE AT LEAST THE MIDDLE AGES, WHERE THERE ARE MANY RECORDS OF PEOPLE EXPOSING THEIR BEHINDS AS AN INSULT. FROM AN ATTACK ON CONSTANTINOPLE DURING THE FOURTH CRUSADE TO A THIRTEENTH CENTURY HUNTING TRIP GONE WRONG, ACCOUNTS OF MOONING AS A FORM OF GLOATING, INSULT, AND JEST ARE PLENTIFUL THROUGHOUT HISTORY.

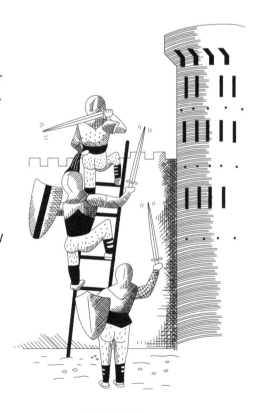

THERE IS EVEN A CASE RECORDED BY HISTORIAN JOSEPHUS FROM THE FIRST CENTURY JEWISH WAR OF A ROMAN SOLDIER EXPOSING HIS BOTTOM AND PRODUCING A **FOUL-SMELLING SOUND** TOWARD THOSE CELEBRATING PASSOVER, CAUSING A BRAWL TO BREAK OUT.

THE ACTUAL TERM **MOONING** SEEMS TO HAVE BEEN COINED AND POPULARIZED AROUND THE 1960s, AS SLANG IN CALIFORNIA. THERE IS EVEN **AN ANNUAL AMTRAK MOONING EVENT** THAT TAKES PLACE IN LAGUNA NIGUEL, CALIFORNIA.

USING A TURN SIGNAL

FLIPPING YOUR DINKER

USING A TURN SIGNAL IS DIVISIVE ACROSS THE BOARD WHEN IT COMES TO DRIVING ETIQUETTE. THOUGH THE LAW REQUIRES DRIVERS TO USE TURN SIGNALS ACROSS THE UNITED STATES, A STUDY BY THE SOCIETY OF AUTOMOTIVE ENGINEERS FOUND THAT AROUND HALF OF DRIVERS CHANGED LANES WITHOUT SIGNALING, AND ABOUT 25 PERCENT MADE TURNS WITHOUT USING THEIR TURN SIGNALS.

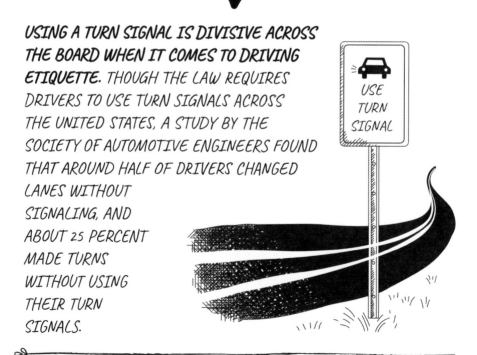

BEFORE CARS HAD TURN SIGNALS, PEOPLE USED **STANDARDIZED HAND SIGNALS.** IT WASN'T LONG BEFORE WE GOT TIRED OF HANGING OUR ARMS OUT OF OUR WINDOWS—ONE OF THE EARLIEST PATENT APPLICATIONS FOR A TURN SIGNAL WAS IN 1907 BY PERCY DOUGLAS-HAMILTON FOR A GADGET FEATURING SIGNAL LIGHTS SHAPED LIKE HANDS.

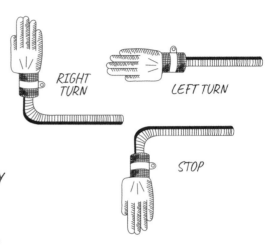

RIGHT TURN

LEFT TURN

STOP

LIKE MOST THINGS, THE TURN SIGNAL DEVELOPED OVER TIME FROM THE CONTRIBUTIONS OF MANY: SILENT FILM STAR **FLORENCE LAWRENCE** FAMOUSLY DEVISED AN AUTO-SIGNALING ARM AS WELL AS A MECHANICAL BRAKE SIGNAL BUT FAILED TO PATENT EITHER. IN 1939 BUICK WAS THE FIRST UNITED STATES COMPANY TO PRODUCE CARS WITH PRE-INSTALLED TURN SIGNALS ON THE REAR LIGHTS. TODAY, THEY ARE STANDARD ON ALL VEHICLES, AND ARE THE SOURCE OF MANY ANGRY TWITTER RANTS.

BUYING A ROUND OF DRINKS

NEXT ONE'S ON ME

BUYING A ROUND OF DRINKS IS A COMMON CUSTOM ON A NIGHT OUT WITH FRIENDS AS A DISPLAY OF COMRADERY AND GOOD SPIRIT.

THERE'S NO RECORD OF WHERE IT ORIGINATED, BUT THE TRADITION IS ESPECIALLY POPULAR IN THE UNITED KINGDOM, IRELAND, AND SCOTLAND.

WRITER AND JOURNALIST WILLIAM GREAVES WROTE A BOOK ON BRITISH PUB CULTURE CALLED **IT'S MY ROUND** AND PUBLISHED AN ETIQUETTE GUIDE FOR ORDERING ROUNDS CALLED **"GREAVES' RULES."**

PUBLISHED IN TODAY NEWSPAPER IN THE 1980s OR '90s, "GREAVES' RULES'" HAVE BECOME A SORT OF **LORE IN PUB CULTURE** AND ARE SAID TO BE FOUND HANGING IN MANY BARS TO THIS DAY. THEY INCLUDE INSTRUCTIONS ON WHO SHOULD ORDER THE FIRST ROUND, AND RULES, LIKE HOW A NEW ROUND MUST BE GRABBED AT THE SIGHT OF A SINGLE EMPTY GLASS.

- THE TRADITION OF -
THE WAVE
A SEA OF CHEER

A CHEERLEADER NAMED KRAZY GEORGE HENDERSON CLAIMS HE INVENTED THE WAVE ON OCTOBER 15, 1981, IN OAKLAND AT A PLAYOFF GAME BETWEEN THE ATHLETICS AND THE NEW YORK YANKEES. THIS GAME WAS ONE OF THE FIRST RECORDED INSTANCES OF THE WAVE, BUT THERE ARE MANY OTHER CLAIMS OF ITS INVENTION THROUGHOUT THE 1970s AND '80s.

HENDERSON'S INVENTION WAS CHALLENGED BY A WAVE LED BY FORMER CHEERLEADER **ROBB WELLER** AT THE UNIVERSITY OF WASHINGTON, BUT THIS TOOK PLACE TWO WEEKS AFTER HENDERSON'S. THE WAVE IS SOMETIMES KNOWN AS **THE MEXICAN WAVE** BECAUSE IT GAINED ATTENTION WHEN BROADCAST DURING THE **1986 WORLD CUP IN MEXICO**.

GEORGE CLAIMED TO HAVE PERFECTED THE WAVE OVER TIME DURING HIS CHEERLEADING CAREER, GETTING THE IDEA FROM A CONSECUTIVE SECTION CHEER DURING HIS TIME AT SAN JOSE STATE AND PRACTICING IT AT **MINOR LEAGUE HOCKEY GAMES** BEFORE THE BIG ONE IN 1981.

- THE TRADITION OF -
STAYING OFF YOUR PHONE AROUND FRIENDS

TALK TO THE ONE YOU'RE WITH

HELLO?

MOST PEOPLE CONSIDER IT RUDE TO BE ON YOUR PHONE AT A SOCIAL FUNCTION, AND THERE'S RESEARCH TO BACK THIS UP: MULTIPLE STUDIES FROM 2014–2018 FOUND THAT USING DEVICES LIKE SMARTPHONES REDUCED THE QUALITY OF SOCIAL INTERACTIONS OR CONVERSATION.

BUT MOST PEOPLE ALSO DO IT THEMSELVES: A 2015 PEW RESEARCH SURVEY FOUND THAT ALTHOUGH 82 PERCENT OF ADULTS SURVEYED SAID CELLPHONES NEGATIVELY IMPACT SOCIAL SETTINGS, 89

WHEN I WAS A YOUNG THING, WE ACTUALLY ENJOYED EACH OTHER'S COMPANY! KIDS THESE DAYS!

PERCENT SAID THEY WERE **GUILTY** OF USING PHONES DURING RECENT SOCIAL ACTIVITY, AND 86 PERCENT SAID SOMEONE ELSE IN THE GROUP DID.

IT'S LIKELY BECOMING THE NORM BECAUSE OF RECIPROCITY: SEEING SOMEONE ELSE DO IT MAKES YOU THINK IT'S ACCEPTABLE. A 2016 STUDY IN COMPUTERS IN HUMAN BEHAVIOR FOUND THAT THOSE WHO PICKED UP THEIR PHONES THE MOST WITH FRIENDS STRUGGLED WITH FEAR OF MISSING OUT (FOMO), SELF-CONTROL, AND COMPULSIVE INTERNET AND SMARTPHONE USE.

- THE TRADITION OF -
THROWING BABY SHOWERS

CELEBRATE LIFE

THE PRECURSORS TO BABY SHOWERS IN ANCIENT TIMES WERE RITUALS THAT TOOK PLACE AFTER THE BIRTH OF A CHILD. IN ANCIENT EGYPT THE SEBOU RITUAL CELEBRATED THE ARRIVAL OF A BABY. SEBOU WAS HELD A WEEK AFTER BIRTH, CELEBRATING THE FACT THAT THE CHILD HAD SURVIVED ITS FIRST SEVEN DAYS OF LIFE.

SEBOU IS STILL CELEBRATED IN EGYPT. IT INVOLVES AN EMPHASIS ON **GENDER** AND MAKING **LOUD NOISES** TO EMBOLDEN THE CHILD'S CHARACTER. IN THE **VICTORIAN ERA,** WOMEN KEPT THEIR PREGNANCIES PRIVATE AND HOSTED TEA PARTIES ONCE THE CHILD WAS BORN FOR OTHER WOMEN TO MEET THE NEW BABY AND BRING GIFTS.

SPILL THE TEA! DID YOU HAVE A BABY?!

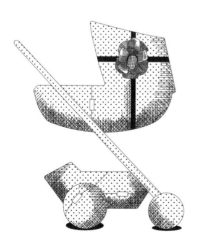

THE MODERN VERSION OF THE BABY SHOWER BEGAN AROUND THE TIME OF THE **BABY BOOM** POST-WORLD WAR II. WITH THE INCREASE OF BIRTHS AND RISE OF CONSUMERISM, BABY SHOWERS SERVED AS A CELEBRATION AND ECONOMIC ADVANTAGE FOR EXPECTING MOTHERS TO RECEIVE MANY ITEMS NEEDED FOR THEIR NEW CHILD.

- THE TRADITION OF -

TIPPING

FIFTEEN OR TWENTY PERCENT?

TIPPING SEEMS TO HAVE STARTED WITH MASTERS GIVING EXTRA MONEY TO SERVANTS *AROUND THE TIME OF TUDOR ENGLAND. BY THE 1700s TIPPING WAS COMMONLY EXPECTED, ESPECIALLY OF VISITING HOUSE GUESTS, AND THERE WERE EVEN EFFORTS TO ABOLISH IT.*

THE PRACTICE WAS BROUGHT FROM EUROPE TO THE UNITED STATES, WHERE IT CONTRIBUTED TO RACIAL OPPRESSION AFTER THE CIVIL WAR. FORMERLY ENSLAVED PEOPLE WERE STILL DISCRIMINATED AGAINST AND ONLY CONSIDERED FOR MENIAL JOBS, AND TIPPING BECAME A WAY TO TAKE ADVANTAGE OF THE WORKERS. MANY WERE PAID **ZERO WAGES** AND RELIED ON SMALL, UNRELIABLE TIPS.

DESPITE SOME LEGAL EFFORTS TO END TIPPING, RESTAURANT OWNERS SAW THE OPPORTUNITY TO GET OUT OF PAYING EMPLOYEES, AND TIPPING SPREAD THROUGHOUT THE SOUTH AND EVENTUALLY TO THE NORTH. TO DATE THERE ARE ONLY **SEVEN STATES** WHERE TIPPED WORKERS RECEIVE A FULL MINIMUM WAGE.

TIP TIP HOORAY! CAFÉ

PRE TIP AMT......... $35.83

TIP I'm a lousy person!

TOTAL

Thank You

- THE TRADITION OF -

DOUBLE TEXTING

MAYBE THEY DIDN'T SEE IT...

WITH ANY NEW TECHNOLOGY, THERE COME NEW SOCIAL NORMS AND RULES. DOUBLE TEXTING IS WHEN YOU FOLLOW UP AN UNANSWERED TEXT WITH ANOTHER ONE. MAGAZINE ARTICLES ACROSS THE WEB OFFER ADVICE ON TEXTING ETIQUETTE AND DETAIL THE RISKS OF DOUBLE TEXTING, WHICH OFTEN COMES OFF AS TOO CLINGY, ESPECIALLY IN DATING SCENARIOS.

BACK WHEN TEXTS WERE
TEN CENTS A MESSAGE
(DEPENDING ON YOUR PLAN),
DOUBLE TEXTING WAS COSTLY
IN MORE THAN JUST THE
SOCIAL SENSE. NOW TEXTING
IS INCREDIBLY ACCESSIBLE.
ABOUT **96 PERCENT** OF
AMERICANS OWN CELL
PHONES, ACCORDING TO A
2019 PEW RESEARCH CENTER STUDY, AND TONS OF CELL PHONE
PLANS BOAST UNLIMITED TEXTING AS PART OF THE DEAL.

WHY HASN'T HE TEXTED ME BACK?!

I'VE SENT HIM 20 TEXTS!

THE CONSENSUS
SEEMS TO BE THAT
SENDING ANOTHER
TEXT IS FINE FOR
A CASUAL REASON
LIKE ADDING MORE
INFORMATION, LETTING
SOMEONE KNOW A
PLAN HAS CHANGED, OR
SENDING A FUNNY MEME.
BUT DOUBLE TEXTING TO PESTER SOMEONE ABOUT WHY THEY
HAVEN'T RESPONDED IS **SURE TO GET YOU LEFT ON READ.**

- THE TRADITION OF -

FLASHING YOUR HEADLIGHTS

ROAD CODE

FLASHING YOUR HEADLIGHTS ON THE ROAD IS A WAY TO COMMUNICATE WITH OTHER DRIVERS, BUT IT TURNS OUT THERE'S A VARIETY OF MESSAGES IT COULD BE SENDING. THE FIRST HEADLIGHTS WERE POWERED BY ACETYLENE IN THE 1880s, SIMILAR TO THE GAS LAMPS USED ON CARRIAGES. RELIABLE ELECTRIC HEADLIGHTS STARTED TO DEVELOP DURING THE 1900s, WITH THE ROUND SEALED BEAM WE RECOGNIZE APPEARING IN 1940.

SOME FLASH THEIR HEADLIGHTS TO WARN DRIVERS OF **UPCOMING HAZARDS** ON THE ROAD, OR TO INFORM A DRIVER THAT THEIR HIGH BEAMS ARE ON. STILL OTHERS USE THE SIGNAL TO NAVIGATE FOUR-WAY STOPS, LET TRUCK DRIVERS KNOW IT'S SAFE TO SWITCH LANES, OR TO WARN FELLOW DRIVERS OF SITTING COPS WITH SPEED GUNS.

STOP!
YOU GO!
COP AHEAD!
TURN YOUR BRIGHTS OFF YOU #%$!

THE ONLY WAY TO EXPRESS MY ROAD RAGE IS THROUGH A LIGHT SHOW!

FLASHING HEADLIGHTS ARE ALSO SOMETIMES USED TO SIGNAL **AGGRESSION** WHILE DRIVING, OR TO TELL A SLOWER CAR TO MOVE OUT OF THE WAY. BECAUSE DIFFERENT REGIONS ALL HAVE DIFFERENT UNDERSTANDINGS OF THE SIGNAL AND SINCE THERE IS NO UNIVERSAL LAW TO CLARIFY, IT MAY BE BEST TO ABSTAIN.

- THE TRADITION OF -

NOT WEARING WHITE AFTER LABOR DAY

FASHION FAUX PAS

ONE OF THE MOST FAMILIAR FASHION FAUX PAS IS THE RULE AGAINST WEARING WHITE AFTER LABOR DAY. THE RULE IS THOUGHT TO COME FROM TIMES BEFORE AIR CONDITIONING, WHEN IT MADE SENSE TO WEAR A LIGHTER COLOR LIKE WHITE DURING THE SUMMER THAT WOULDN'T ATTRACT SO MUCH HEAT.

WHITE CLOTHES COULD BE MORE LIKELY TO BE SOILED BY BAD WEATHER AS THE COLDER MONTHS APPROACHED, MAKING THE RULE FAIRLY PRACTICAL. SOME THEORIZE THAT IT WAS ALSO A MOVE OF **ELITISM** ON BEHALF OF THE WEALTHY.

WHITE CLOTHING COULD HAVE BEEN ASSOCIATED WITH **LEISURELY VACATION WEAR,** DISTINGUISHING THOSE WHO COULD AFFORD TO GO AWAY FOR THE SUMMER. SWITCHING TO DARKER COLORS PROBABLY MARKED A RETURN TO THE

CITIES AND A CHANGE IN THE SEASONS. TODAY, WITH **WINTER WHITES** HAVING A BIG MOMENT, THE RULE IS RARELY FOLLOWED.

- THE TRADITION OF -

RECYCLING

WASTE NOT, WANT NOT

HUMANS HAVE BEEN RECYCLING LONG BEFORE THE GREEN MOVEMENT OF THE 1970s. IN ANCIENT AND PREINDUSTRIAL TIMES, IT MADE SENSE TO REPAIR AND REPURPOSE ITEMS THAT WEREN'T SO EASY TO REPLACE, ESPECIALLY IF YOU WERE RESPONSIBLE FOR DISPOSING OF YOUR OWN TRASH. IN JAPAN, THERE ARE RECORDS OF PAPER BEING RECYCLED AS EARLY AS 1031.

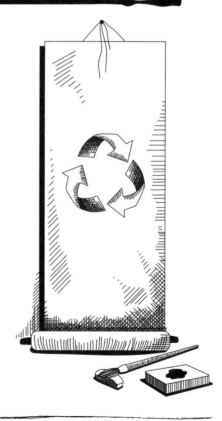

PAPER RECYCLING IN THE COLONIES BEGAN AS EARLY AS 1690 AT THE **RITTENHOUSE MILL IN PHILADELPHIA,** AND SCRAP-METAL YARDS COLLECTED EVERYTHING FROM TIN TO KETTLES TO SUPPORT THE **REVOLUTIONARY WAR EFFORT.** LEADING INTO THE VICTORIAN ERA, **RAGMEN** COLLECTED OLD RAGS FROM HOUSES TO TURN INTO PAPER, AND WOMEN OFTEN HAD THEIR DRESSES ALTERED TO REFLECT NEW STYLES, RATHER THAN BUY A NEW ONE.

WHEN THE **GREAT DEPRESSION** HIT, RECYCLING AND REUSING MATERIALS WAS MORE OF A NECESSITY THAN EVER. WORLD WAR II SAW THE SALVAGING OF EVERYTHING FROM **KITCHEN FAT** TO **NYLONS** TO HELP THE WAR EFFORT. SINCE THE 1960s THE VALUE OF RECYCLING HAS PIVOTED FROM OUR NEED TO REUSE TO OUR NEED TO MANAGE **EXCESSIVE WASTE.**

- THE TRADITION OF -

SENDING THANK-YOU NOTES

A NICE TOUCH

LETTERS OF THANKS AND GOODWILL HAVE BEEN AROUND AS LONG AS WRITING ITSELF. THE ANCIENT EGYPTIANS EVEN WROTE LETTERS TO THE DEAD ALONGSIDE OFFERINGS, EXPRESSING GRATITUDE AND WISHING THEM WELL IN THE AFTERLIFE.

WHEN THE FIRST POSTAGE STAMP KNOWN AS THE **PENNY BLACK** WAS ISSUED IN 1840 IN WHAT WAS THEN ENGLAND, IT BECAME EASIER THAN EVER TO SEND LETTERS. THE POST OFFICE IS A VITAL INSTITUTION AND IS INCLUDED IN THE US CONSTITUTION (ARTICLE 1, SECTION 8).

A 2018 STUDY PUBLISHED IN PSYCHOLOGICAL SCIENCE INVOLVED PARTICIPANTS WRITING LETTERS OF GRATITUDE TO OTHERS AND FOUND THAT NOT ONLY DID THE WRITERS FEEL BETTER AFTERWARDS, BUT **THEY ALSO UNDERESTIMATED HOW POSITIVELY THE RECIPIENTS RESPONDED TO THE GESTURE.**

DRIVING ON THE RIGHT SIDE OF THE ROAD

ARE WE DOING THIS WRONG?

IT IS BELIEVED THAT AS EARLY AS ANCIENT TIMES IT WAS THE NORM TO TRAVEL ON THE LEFT SIDE OF THE ROAD. SINCE MOST PEOPLE ARE RIGHT-HANDED, TRAVELING ON THE LEFT ALLOWED THEM TO USE A WEAPON IN THEIR DOMINANT HAND WHETHER THEY WERE A DRIVER DEFENDING A CARRIAGE OR WIELDING A SWORD ON HORSEBACK.

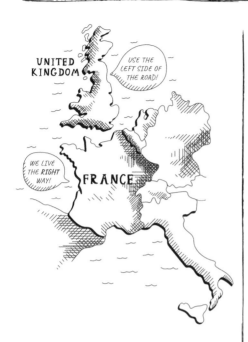

IN 1773 THE BRITISH GOVERNMENT PASSED THE GENERAL HIGHWAYS ACT, OFFICIALLY ADVISING PEOPLE TO USE THE LEFT SIDE OF THE ROAD. IN **FRANCE** THEY PREFERRED THE RIGHT, AND MANY FORMER COLONIES OF EACH COUNTRY STILL FOLLOW THEIR RESPECTIVE PREFERENCE TO THIS DAY.

IN THE UNITED STATES, FAVORING THE RIGHT SIDE CAN BE CREDITED TO THE FREIGHT WAGONS OF THE LATE 1700s. PULLED BY **TEAMS OF HORSES**, THE FREIGHT WAGONS DIDN'T HAVE DRIVERS' SEATS, SO THE DRIVER SAT ON THE BACK LEFT HORSE AND CONTROLLED THE REST WITH REINS IN THEIR RIGHT HAND. WHEN HENRY FORD RELEASED THE WILDLY POPULAR **MODEL T** WITH THE STEERING WHEEL ON THE LEFT SIDE, THE CHOICE WAS CEMENTED.

- THE TRADITION OF -
NOT DISCUSSING MONEY

KEEPING YOUR WALLET TO YOURSELF

BLECH! SUCH A VULGARIAN!

SHAKESPEARE'S THE MERCHANT OF VENICE EXPLORES THE PRINCIPLES OF WEALTH, SPENDING, AND THE VALUES THEY REPRESENT. MANY OF SHAKESPEARE'S PLAYS ARE RIFE WITH CAUTIONARY ADVICE ABOUT THE BURDEN OF MONEY'S POWER. THOUGH THE TOPIC MAY HAVE BEEN FAIR GAME FOR ELIZABETHAN STAGES, IN WESTERN CULTURE TODAY IT'S OFTEN THOUGHT THAT DISCUSSING MONEY IS IN POOR TASTE.

IN HER 1922 BOOK ETIQUETTE IN SOCIETY, IN BUSINESS, IN POLITICS, AND AT HOME, **EMILY POST** WRITES "ONE WHO IS RICH DOES NOT MAKE A DISPLAY OF HIS MONEY OR HIS

POSSESSIONS. ONLY A **VULGARIAN** TALKS CEASELESSLY ABOUT HOW MUCH THIS OR THAT COST HIM." IT'S POSSIBLE THAT THIS ATTITUDE WAS ENCOURAGED BY CAPITALISM'S INDUSTRIAL BOOM OF THE 1800s AND 1900s.

A WEALTHY PERSON MAY HAVE THE LUXURY TO VIEW TALKING ABOUT MONEY AS CRASS, BUT FOR MEMBERS OF THE MIDDLE AND LOWER CLASSES, ***DISCUSSING WAGES WITH OTHERS CAN BE A WAY TO ENSURE EQUITY IN PAY.*** BECAUSE DISCUSSING MONEY CAN LEAD TO INFORMED WORKERS, KEEPING THE SUBJECT TABOO CAN BENEFIT GATEKEEPERS OF THE UPPER CLASS.

- THE TRADITION OF -

XOXO

KISSES AND HUGS

WHEN YOU SEE AN *X* AND AN *O* AT THE END OF A LETTER, YOU KNOW IT SIGNIFIES KISSES AND HUGS. SOME SPECULATE THAT THE SYMBOLS GOT THEIR MEANING BECAUSE *X* RESEMBLES A KISS AND *O* RESEMBLES AN EMBRACE OF ARMS, BUT THE MARKS MOST LIKELY HAVE ROOTS IN CHRISTIANITY.

AN **X** REPRESENTED THE CROSS AND THE GREEK WORD FOR CHRIST, χριστός. DURING THE MIDDLE AGES MANY **COULD NOT WRITE,** SO IT WAS COMMON TO SIGN A DOCUMENT WITH AN X. THEY WOULD THEN SEAL THE SIGNATURE WITH A KISS, WHICH PROBABLY LED TO X AND A KISS BECOMING SYNONYMOUS IN WRITING.

OOOOOOOOOOOOH BEAUTIFUL FOR SPACIOUS SKIES!

SIGN IT WITH AN 'O'

SIGN IT WITH AN X! AND SEAL IT WITH A KISS!

THE ORIGIN OF **O** IS A LITTLE MORE UNCLEAR: SOME BELIEVE THAT O WAS USED AS A SIGNATURE BY **JEWISH IMMIGRANTS** WHO WERE ILLITERATE ONCE THEY ARRIVED IN THE UNITED STATES, AS AN ALTERNATIVE TO THE CHRISTIAN X. MAYBE THE ACCOMPANIMENT OF X AND O IN THE GAME OF TICK-TAC-TOE INSPIRED TYING THE TWO TOGETHER.

WAITING THREE DAYS TO CALL

THE THREE-DAY RULE

THERE ARE TONS OF ARBITRARY RULES SURROUNDING DATING, AND THE THREE-DAY RULE IS ONE OF THE MOST FAMILIAR. THE RULE STATES ONE SHOULD WAIT THREE DAYS TO CALL A ROMANTIC INTEREST, SO AS NOT TO APPEAR DESPERATE. THERE'S NO SIGN OF WHO CAME UP WITH IT, BUT IT SEEMS TO HAVE BECOME POPULAR AROUND THE LATE 1990s TO EARLY 2000s.

THE THREE-DAY RULE IS REFERENCED IN POPULAR MEDIA AND ROMCOMS THROUGHOUT THIS TIME. THERE IS AN EPISODE OF *HOW I MET YOUR MOTHER* NAMED "THE THREE DAYS RULE," AND THE 1996 COMEDY FAVORITE *SWINGERS* FEATURES A SCENE IN WHICH THE TWO LEADS DEBATE **HOW MANY DAYS** THEY SHOULD WAIT TO CALL AFTER A DATE.

NOW, THIS RULE HAS MOSTLY FALLEN OUT OF FASHION. IT'S MOST LIKELY BECAUSE OF A PREFERENCE FOR HONESTY OVER PLAYING GAMES, AND DUE TO THE RISE OF CASUAL COMMUNICATION VIA TEXT AND SOCIAL MEDIA. THESE PLATFORMS GIVE US MORE OPTIONS FOR CONTACTING A POTENTIAL PARTNER— ONES THAT ARE FAR MORE APPEALING THAN **WAITING BY THE PHONE.**

- THE TRADITION OF -
BACHELOR AND BACHELORETTE PARTIES

LAST NIGHT STAG

BACHELOR PARTIES ARE THOUGHT TO BE TRACED BACK TO THE FIFTH CENTURY BC IN ANCIENT GREECE. SPARTANS ARE SAID TO HAVE HOSTED DINNERS ON THE FINAL NIGHT BEFORE A GROOM'S WEDDING IN HIS HONOR.

ALSO KNOWN AS **STAG PARTIES,** MODERN BACHELOR PARTIES LIKELY GOT THEIR WILD CONNOTATION FROM A FAMOUS ONE THROWN IN 1896 BY HERBERT BARNUM SEELEY, GRANDSON OF CIRCUS-MAN P. T. BARNUM. THE PARTY WAS RAIDED BY POLICE BECAUSE OF A NUDE PERFORMANCE BY A DANCER AND WAS DUBBED **"THE AWFUL SEELEY DINNER."**

BACHELORETTE PARTIES AND, AS THEY'RE CALLED IN THE UNITED KINGDOM AND IRELAND, **HEN NIGHTS** SEEM TO HAVE POPPED UP BETWEEN THE 1960s AND 1980s, SPURRED BY THE SEXUAL REVOLUTION.

WOMEN WERE LIKELY GOING OUT TO CELEBRATE AFTER BRIDAL SHOWERS FOR SIMILAR PURPOSES LONG BEFORE. THE ACTUAL TERM *BACHELORETTE* WAS FIRST PUBLISHED IN *THE NEW YORK TIMES* IN 1981.

- THE TRADITION OF -

SALUTING

TIP YOUR CAP

A POPULAR THEORY CLAIMS THAT THE SALUTE COMES FROM KNIGHTS *LIFTING THE VISORS ON THEIR HELMETS WHEN APPROACHING OTHERS. BY REVEALING THEIR FACES, THEY COULD BE IDENTIFIED BY SUPERIORS, OR COMMUNICATE PEACEFUL INTENTIONS. SALUTING COULD ALSO HAVE BEEN A GREETING TO SHOW THAT ONE WAS NOT HOLDING A WEAPON IN THEIR HAND.*

I COMETH IN PEACE! SHOW THY MUG!

THE GESTURE SIMILARLY COULD HAVE EVOLVED FROM **REMOVING ONE'S HAT AS A SIGN OF RESPECT,** A COMMON PRACTICE IN THE BRITISH ARMY. TO SAVE THE EFFORT OF TAKING ONE'S HAT OFF COMPLETELY EVERY TIME ONE PASSED A SUPERIOR, TOUCHING THE HAND TO THE HAT BECAME AN ACCEPTABLE ALTERNATIVE.

OPTION 1   OPTION 2

A PASSAGE IN A BRITISH ORDER BOOK FROM AS EARLY AS 1745 INSTRUCTS "THE MEN ARE ORDERED NOT TO PULL OFF THEIR HATS WHEN THEY PASS AN OFFICER, OR TO SPEAK TO THEM, BUT ONLY TO CLAP UP THEIR HANDS TO THEIR HATS AND BOW AS THEY PASS." ANOTHER THEORY CLAIMS THAT THE PALMS-DOWN SALUTE WAS FAVORED TO HIDE THE **DIRTY PALMS OF SAILORS IN THE BRITISH NAVY.**

I SEE YOU... I HEAR YOU... I RESPECT YOU.

BATHING REGULARLY

KEEPING IT CLEAN

BATHING HAS BEEN A SIGNIFICANT AND DEFINING ASPECT OF CULTURE SINCE ANCIENT TIMES. ANCIENT EGYPTIANS PLACED AN EMPHASIS ON APPEARANCE AND HYGIENE, REGULARLY WEARING COSMETICS, PERFUMES, OILS, AND CREAMS. THEY BATHED DAILY AND OFTEN WASHED THEIR FEET AND HANDS AFTER MEALS.

IN ANCIENT ROME, BATHING WAS SUPPORTED BY THEIR INNOVATIVE AQUEDUCT SYSTEMS. **PUBLIC BATHS** TOOK PRIORITY OVER PRIVATE PLUMBING, AND BATHS, WHICH SERVED AS AN IMPORTANT SOCIAL HUB, WERE VISITED ON A NEAR DAILY BASIS.

MOHENJO-DARO, AN ANCIENT CIVILIZATION IN THE INDUS VALLEY, FEATURES NO TEMPLES OR MONUMENTS BUT HAS ONE OF THE EARLIEST PUBLIC BATHS IN HISTORY. THE CITY FEATURES INFRASTRUCTURE CENTERED AROUND CLEANLINESS, WITH BATHROOMS AND DRAINAGE SYSTEMS IN ALMOST EVERY HOME IMPLYING THAT REGULAR BATHING MAY HAVE BEEN AROUND SINCE 2500 BC.

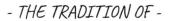

- THE TRADITION OF -

SERVICE DOGS

HUMANS' BEST FRIEND

IT WAS SOMEWHERE AROUND TWENTY TO FORTY THOUSAND YEARS AGO WHEN WOLVES WERE DOMESTICATED INTO OUR DOG COMPANIONS. IN ISRAEL, REMAINS WERE FOUND IN AN APPROXIMATELY 12,000-YEAR-OLD NATUFIAN GRAVE OF A PERSON BURIED WITH THEIR HAND ON THEIR DOG. TODAY MANY DOGS PROVIDE PSYCHIATRIC HELP, EMOTIONAL SUPPORT, AND AID FOR THOSE WITH DISABILITIES OR MEDICAL CONDITIONS.

AN ANCIENT ROMAN FRESCO FOUND AT THE SITE OF HERCULANEUM FROM THE FIRST CENTURY AD DEPICTS A DOG LEADING A BLIND MAN. SIMILAR IMAGES ARE FOUND ON CHINESE SCROLLS FROM THE THIRTEENTH CENTURY. IN ANCIENT EGYPT, DOGS WERE REGARDED AND BURIED WITH GREAT RESPECT. WALL PAINTINGS SHOW MEN WALKING DOGS WITH COLLARS AND LEASHES, AND RECOVERED LEATHER COLLARS SHOW ENDEARING NAMES RANGING FROM **BRAVE ONE** TO **USELESS**.

STANDARDIZED TRAINING FOR GUIDE DOGS TOOK SHAPE IN THE LATE 1700s, AND TOOK OFF IN GERMANY TO HELP SOLDIERS BLINDED BY MUSTARD GAS IN THE AFTERMATH OF **WORLD WAR I**. THE SEEING EYE ORGANIZATION FOUNDED BY DOROTHY EUSTIS PLEDGED TO PROVIDE SERVICE DOGS FOR BLINDED VETERANS ON THE DAY AFTER THE ATTACK ON PEARL HARBOR. GUIDE DOGS BECAME AN INVALUABLE RESOURCE FOR VETERANS POST-WORLD WAR II AND CONTINUE TO SERVE CITIZENS ALL OVER THE WORLD.

- THE TRADITION OF -
CELEBRATING BIRTHDAYS
ANOTHER YEAR FOR THE BOOKS

THE BIBLE REFERENCES A PHARAOH'S BIRTHDAY CELEBRATION IN ANCIENT EGYPT AROUND 3000 BC, BUT IT IS BELIEVED TO BE A FESTIVAL COMMEMORATING HIS CORONATION DATE AS A GOD-KING. MANY BELIEVE THE CUSTOM OF BLOWING OUT CANDLES ON A BIRTHDAY CAKE COMES FROM THE **ANCIENT GREEKS** OFFERING A MOON-SHAPED CAKE WITH LIT CANDLES TO THE GODDESS OF THE HUNT AND MOON, **ARTEMIS.**

EIGHTEENTH CENTURY GERMAN BIRTHDAY CELEBRATION **KINDERFESTE** INVOLVED GIVING A CHILD A BIRTHDAY CAKE WITH A CANDLE FOR EACH YEAR OF THEIR LIFE, PLUS ONE KNOWN AS THE *LIGHT OF LIFE* TO REPRESENT HOPE FOR THE NEXT YEAR.

IN KOREA, *DOL* IS A CELEBRATION OF A BABY'S FIRST BIRTHDAY, WHICH WAS A MILESTONE WHEN SURVIVAL RATES WERE LOW DUE TO DISEASE. THE BABIES, WHO ARE PRESENTED WITH AMPLE FOOD, PICK AN OBJECT OFF OF A TABLE TO DETERMINE THEIR FUTURE PROFESSION. THE **100-DAY CELEBRATION** SIMILARLY MARKS A CHILD'S SURVIVAL AND IS PRACTICED THROUGHOUT ASIA.

- THE TRADITION OF -

DRINKING COFFEE AND TEA

THE GIFT OF CAFFEINE

FOR MANY PEOPLE TODAY IT'S HARD TO IMAGINE LIFE WITHOUT A DAILY CUP OF COFFEE OR TEA (OR SEVEN). AN ETHIOPIAN LEGEND TELLS OF A GOATHERD NAMED **KALDI** WHO DISCOVERED COFFEE WHEN HIS GOATS DANCED WITH ENERGY AFTER EATING THE RED BERRIES OFF OF A BUSH.

WHILE THE TRADITION WAS LIKELY BROUGHT FROM ETHIOPIA, THERE IS NO SURVIVING EVIDENCE OF COFFEE DRINKING UNTIL THE FIFTEENTH CENTURY IN WHAT IS NOW YEMEN IN SOUTHERN ARABIA, WHERE IT WAS BREWED AND DRANK IN **SUFI MONASTERIES.**

TEA IS SAID TO HAVE BEEN DISCOVERED BY **CHINESE EMPEROR SHEN NUNG** WHEN LEAVES FROM A TEA BUSH BLEW INTO HIS POT OF BOILING WATER. HIS MEDICAL ENCYCLOPEDIA PEN TS'AO DATED TO 2737 BC DETAILS THE BENEFITS OF CAFFEINE IN TEA, INCLUDING THAT **"IT GLADDENS AND CHEERS THE HEART."**

- THE TRADITION OF -
TATTOOING
BODY ART

WE KNOW HUMANS HAVE BEEN TATTOOING THEIR BODIES SINCE AT LEAST 5,300 YEARS AGO, THANKS TO THE DISCOVERY OF A MAN FOUND MUMMIFIED IN THE ICE OF THE ALPS. HIS BODY HAS SIXTY-ONE TATTOOS IN TOTAL, BELIEVED TO BE THERAPEUTIC, AS THEY ALIGN WITH CLASSIC ACUPUNCTURE POINTS. MUMMIFIED REMAINS YIELDING EVIDENCE OF TATTOOS IN ANCIENT CULTURES HAVE BEEN FOUND ALL OVER, FROM PERU TO CHINA.

THIS ONE HAS FADED A BIT OVER TIME...

TATTOOS HAVE BEEN FOUND ON ANCIENT EGYPTIAN FEMALE MUMMIES DATING BACK TO 2000 BC, AND FIGURINES CIRCA 4000 BC DEPICT WOMEN WITH TATTOOS AS WELL. THE REMAINS OF A FIFTH-CENTURY SIBERIAN ICE MAIDEN KNOWN AS **PRINCESS OF UKOK** FEATURE SOME OF THE MOST COMPLEX AND ARTISTIC MUMMIFIED TATTOOS EVER FOUND, CHARACTERISTIC OF THE PAZYRYK PEOPLE.

BOTH THE INDIGENOUS PEOPLE OF AMERICA AND AUSTRONESIAN PEOPLES PRACTICED ELABORATE TATTOOING. **POLYNESIAN CULTURE** IS SAID TO GIVE US THE VERY WORD TATTOO, ADOPTED FROM TAHITIAN ISLANDERS' TERM **TATATAU** OR **TATTAU**. TATTOOS IN EACH OF THESE ANCIENT CULTURES REPRESENTED EVERYTHING FROM RELIGION AND SOCIAL STANDING TO PERSONAL ADORNMENT AND EXPRESSION.

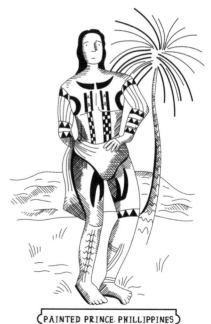

PAINTED PRINCE, PHILLIPPINES

SMILING IN PHOTOGRAPHS

SAY CHEESE

IT WASN'T ALWAYS SECOND NATURE TO SMILE OR SAY CHEESE IN PHOTOGRAPHS. IN THE EARLY DAYS OF PHOTOGRAPHY, A SERIOUS FACIAL EXPRESSION WAS STANDARD. MANY BELIEVE SOMBER LOOKS WERE EASIER TO HOLD FOR EARLY CAMERAS WITH LONG EXPOSURE TIMES, YET THE TREND ENDURED EVEN AS TECHNOLOGY ADVANCED TO A QUICKER CAPTURE IN THE LATE 1800s.

ANOTHER THEORY BLAMES **DENTAL HYGIENE**—THOUGH IT WAS COMMON TO HAVE UNSIGHTLY OR MISSING TEETH DURING THE VICTORIAN ERA, A CLOSE-LIPPED PHOTO MIGHT HAVE SEEMED MORE ATTRACTIVE. ULTIMATELY, HOWEVER, THE TREND CAN BE ATTRIBUTED TO THE SOCIAL ETIQUETTE OF THE TIME.

AS A PRIM AND CONTROLLED DEMEANOR WAS CONSIDERED PROPER, A WIDE SMILE IN A PHOTO COULD BE SEEN AS UNREFINED OR CHILDISH. IN THE DAYS OF PAINTINGS, EXPENSIVE PORTRAITS AIMED FOR ELEGANCE AND FORMALITY, AND EARLY PHOTOGRAPHS FOLLOWED SUIT. AS PHOTOGRAPHY BECAME LESS EXPENSIVE AND MORE ACCESSIBLE TO ALL, **SMILES WERE WELCOMED.**

- THE TRADITION OF -

WEARING BATHING SUITS

DIVE IN

BEFORE BATHING SUITS, PEOPLE SWAM NAKED OR IN THEIR UNDERWEAR. IN THE 1700s, MEN WORE SHORTS AND WOMEN WORE BATHING GOWNS USUALLY MADE OF WOOL OR FLANNEL. THEY OFTEN WEIGHTED DOWN THE HEMS TO PREVENT THE WATER FROM REVEALING THEIR LEGS.

THROUGHOUT THE 1800s IT WAS COMMON FOR WOMEN TO WEAR SUITS THAT FEATURED SHORTER-SLEEVED DRESSES WITH BLOOMERS BENEATH, OFTEN ACCOMPANIED BY BLACK STOCKINGS AND BATHING SLIPPERS. IT WAS CONSIDERED INDECENT EXPOSURE IN 1907, WHEN SWIMMER AND ACTRESS **ANNETTE KELLERMAN** WAS ARRESTED FOR DEBUTING A ONE-PIECE SUIT WITH SHORTS SHOWING HER LEGS ON REVERE BEACH.

SOME BEACHES HAD CENSORS WHO MEASURED THE LENGTH OF WOMEN'S SUITS, BUT SWIMWEAR ONLY CONTINUED TO GET SHORTER AND TIGHTER UNTIL 1946 WHEN **MICHELINE BERNARDINI** MODELED **LOUIS RÉARD'S** REINVENTION OF THE BIKINI. RÉARD'S DESIGN MAY HAVE SEEMED SHOCKING, BUT **ANCIENT ROMAN MOSAICS** FROM THE FOURTH CENTURY AD DEPICT WOMEN WEARING BIKINI-LIKE TWO-PIECES AS SPORTSWEAR.

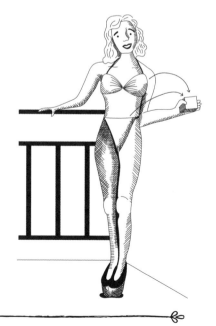

ACKNOWLEDGMENTS

A big thank you to my parents, **Jim** and **Kyung**, as well as to **John Whalen** and **Whalen Book Works** for the opportunity to write this book. My gratitude goes to **Rebecca Pry** for bringing this book to life with her brilliant illustrations, and to designer **Melissa Gerber**, editor **Margaret McGuire Novak**, and copy editor **Davene Wasser** for bringing it all together. And finally thanks to you, for keeping the everyday behavior of reading alive.

ABOUT THE AUTHOR

Laura Hetherington is a writer and actress living in New York City. She received a BA in English from Fordham University and enjoys finding the poetry and humor in everyday life. She has a love for ceramics, a good hike, and her guitar Zoe. Find her on Instagram @laura.heth.

ABOUT THE ILLUSTRATOR

Rebecca Pry is an illustrator and designer living in Warwick, New York. She received a BFA in Illustration from Rhode Island School of Design in 2013. Rebecca's art adds a humorous twist to everyday items and scenes, and she has created patterns and graphics for home goods, books, accessories, apparel, and regularly shows her work in local galleries in the Hudson Valley. When she is not drawing, she is outside in a brightly colored sweater. See more at rebeccapry.com.

ABOUT WHALEN BOOK WORKS

PUBLISHING PRACTICAL & CREATIVE NONFICTION

Whalen Book Works is a small, independent book publishing company based in Kennebunkport, Maine, that combines top-notch design, unique formats, and fresh content to create truly innovative gift books.

Our unconventional approach to bookmaking is a close-knit, creative, and collaborative process among authors, artists, designers, editors, and booksellers. We publish a small, carefully curated list each season, and we take the time to make each book exactly what it needs to be.

We believe in giving back. That's why we plant one tree for every ten books we print. Your purchase supports a tree in the United States National Parks.

Get in touch! ⤷

Visit us at **WhalenBookWorks.com**

or write to us at
68 North Street, Kennebunkport, ME 04046.